How to Become a Civil Servant

Orders: Please contact www.How2Become.com

ISBN: 978-1-912370-89-4

First published 2021

Copyright © 2021 How2Become.com.

All Rights Reserved. For personal use only.

Disclaimer:

IMPORTANT: All resources, products, content, and training from How2Become is intended for educational use only, as an aid to help you prepare and come up with your own honest answers. How2Become is not acting in conjunction with, or associated with, any third-party organisation.

How2Become and its sites are not responsible for anyone failing any part of any selection process as a result of the information contained within its content, products, website, resources, and videos. How2Become and their authors cannot accept any responsibility for any errors or omissions within these resources, however, caused. No responsibility for loss or damage occasioned by any person acting, or refraining from action, as a result of the material can be accepted by How2Become.

All rights reserved. Apart from any permitted use under UK copyright law no part of this publication may be reproduced or transmitted in any form or by any means, electronic or mechanical, including photocopying, recording, or any information, storage or retrieval system without permission in writing from the publisher or under licence from the Copyright Licensing Agency Limited. Further details of such licenses (for reprographic reproduction) may be obtained from the Copyright Licensing Agency Ltd, Saffron House, 6-10 Kirby Street, London EC1N 8TS.

Contents

The Civil Service Success Profiles 5

The Civil Service Interview 13

Situational Judgement Test 123

Civil Service Situational Judgement Test 1 141

Civil Service Situational Judgement Test 2 165

Civil Service Situational Judgement Test 3 209

Numerical Reasoning Test 251

Civil Service Numerical Reasoning Test 1 265

Civil Service Numerical Reasoning Test 2 277

Civil Service Numerical Reasoning Test 3 293

Verbal Reasoning Test 307

Civil Service Verbal Reasoning Test 1 323

Civil Service Verbal Reasoning Test 2 343

Civil Service Verbal Reasoning Test 3 367

The Civil Service
Success Profiles

When you apply for a role within the Civil Service, you will be assessed against a set criteria which is relevant to the role you are applying for. This set criteria are commonly known as the Civil Service Success Profiles. This replaced the previous competency framework used by the Civil Service. The previous competency framework assessed candidates for all roles on the same set of competencies. This was deemed ineffective as not all of the competencies were relevant to the role being applied for. With the Civil Success Profiles candidates are only assessed on the profiles which are relevant to the role.

The Civil Service Success Profiles are split into a number of different sections, these are as follows.

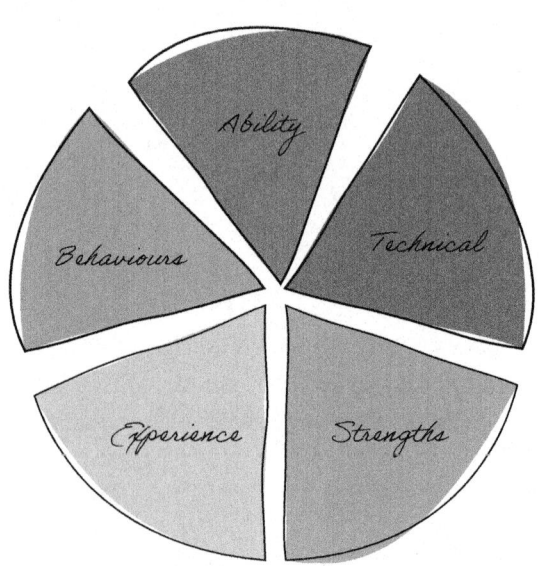

The Civil Service Success Profiles

Ability: This is used to assess candidate's performance in a number of different ways such as online assessment tests, ie Numerical, Verbal and Situational Judgement tests. The number of tests, you will face would be dependent on the role being applied for. If the role is of a technical nature you may have to undertake further tests to test your technical job-related ability.

Technical: The candidate will have to display specific job related knowledge and skills and divulge any relevant and required qualifications.

Experience: Previous experience gained through previous roles related to the role you are applying for.

Strengths: These are based on what we do on a regular basis, what we excel at and how they motivate us. These are not so much on how you perform at work, but what you enjoy doing. This ensures that the role is as much a good fit for the candidate as well as the employer. The thinking is that if the role is matched to something you enjoy you will more likely perform to an exceptional standard. In total there are 36 strengths that you can be assessed against, and are listed in what is known as the Civil Service Strengths Dictionary. You will only be assessed against the strengths which are deemed as a requirement for the role.

- **Adaptable:** You are able to adapt to different work situations or environments and your competence to perform your duties is not impacted.

- **Analytical:** When making decisions you analyse all the information comprehensively so your decision is based on the best evidence available.

- **Authentic:** You have self-awareness and are true to yourself even when in pressurised situations.

- **Catalyst:** You have high levels of self-motivation when it comes to achieving goals. You are confident in using your own initiative when taking action.

- **Challenger:** You bring fresh perspectives to any situations. You are able to see other people's views and understand there are many different viewpoints to consider.

- **Change Agent:** You embrace change and are positive when leading and showing support to others with change.

- **Confident:** You are able to take charge of situations, others and decisions. You communicate in a confident manner and give direction where necessary.

- **Courageous:** You are innovative, who will try new approaches and happy to push yourself to work outside your comfort zone.

The Civil Service Success Profiles

- **Decisive:** You use sound judgement and a considered approach to situations and tasks when making decisions.

- **Disciplined:** You follow process and guidelines. You always operate exclusively to set guidelines and standards.

- **Efficient:** You turn resources into results in the most economical and efficient way possible.

- **Emotionally Intelligent:** You are able to draw insight from your emotions and others to demonstrate high levels of empathy.

- **Enabler:** You are able to see potential in everyone and encourage them to develop and progress.

- **Explainer:** You can communicate your thoughts and ideas with ease verbally or in writing. You are able to adapt your communication to suit the audience.

- **Focussed:** You always strive for quality outcomes in all that you do.

- **Inclusive:** You are able to see recognise everyone as an individual. You accept people for who they are and treat everyone fair and equally. You encourage others to share their ideas and provide opportunities to contribute.

- **Influencer:** You are able to influence others to get their agreement.

- **Improver:** You are always looking for new ways of doing things and enjoy coming up with fresh ideas.

- **Learner:** You always seek new information and will always look for continuous change for self-development.

- **Mediator:** You provide a stable platform for teams, being able to provide a common ground and goal. You thrive within a team environment, diving forward a shared objective.

- **Mission:** You are pursuant of objectives which give a sense of meaning and purpose, which work towards a longer-term goal.

- **Motivator:** You are able to motivate others with ease to move things along at an accepted pace and can makes things happen.

- **Negotiator:** You are able to facilitate discussion with the goal of getting everyone involved to reach an agreement.

- **Networker:** You are able to start and maintain professional relationships with others from within the organisation and external stakeholders.

- **Organiser:** You always plan ahead and are well prepared. You manage your time to maximise productivity and efficiency.

- **Precise:** You are focused on all details to ensure all is accurate and with no mistakes.

- **Preventer:** You are a forward thinker and will always assess risk to identify and prevent any issues before they occur.

- **Problem Solver:** You are always positive when faced with issues and identifying possible solutions.

- **Relationship Builder:** You are able to quickly establish trust and a mutual respect with others.

- **Resilient:** You are a composed individual, who will not dwell on setbacks and will always learn from them.

- **Responsible:** You take ownership for your decisions and are always accountable for what you have stated you will deliver.

- **Service Focussed:** You seek ways to serve your customer, always putting their needs first.

- **Strategic:** You are able to see the bigger picture and be considerate of the wider factor and implications of decisions made.

- **Team Leader:** You can effectively lead a team with professionalism and confidence. You encourage team spirit, whilst considering everyone's individual needs.
- **Team Player:** You work well within a team and endeavour to ensure the team functions correctly and is effective.
- **Visionary:** You build and share a clear vision of the future.

Behaviours: In total, there are nine behaviours that form the basis of all job roles. In order to perform to a high standard, you should learn and understand the behaviours prior to attending your interview. A brief description and explanation of each of the nine Civil Service behaviours are provided below to help you. It is worth noting that on the job description for the role, it is often stated which behaviours you will be assessed against during the selection process.

The Civil Service Interview

SEEING THE BIG PICTURE

When answering interview questions that are based on seeing the big picture, you must show that you understand exactly how your job position fits into the Civil Service and its goals. You also must show your awareness of how the work you are doing is focused on the wider good of the nation.

CHANGING AND IMPROVING

In your answers to questions that assess your ability to improve and change, you must show that you are capable of coming up with new and creative ways to solve problems and improve your own and your team's performance. You must show that you are capable of constantly reviewing your performance and periodically asking for, and responding to, feedback from others.

MAKING EFFECTIVE DECISIONS

It is important you use information and data to make accurate decisions whilst working in the Civil Service. This is far more effective than taking unnecessary risks or simply going on gut feeling! When making decisions, show that you consider the options and the likely outcome.

LEADERSHIP

As a leader within the Civil Service you must show a passion for delivering excellent public services. You must motivate, inspire and direct others to achieve the objectives of the Civil Service. In everything you do, you must value diversity, you must operate in a fair and respectful manner, and must value and respect other people's contributions whilst creating opportunities for all.

COMMUNICATING AND INFLUENCING

Whilst communicating in an organisation such as the Civil Service, you need to use clarity, confidence, purpose and an enthusiastic tone. When communicating with others, show that you are respectful of their views and you take into consideration their needs.

WORKING TOGETHER

Within the Civil Service you will need to work alongside other internal members, other departments and external contractors and stakeholders. Therefore, teamwork is an essential skill needed within all roles. In your answers to the 'working together' interview questions, show you have the ability to work with everyone, regardless of their background, views or opinions.

DEVELOPING SELF AND OTHERS

Continuous learning and development are vital aspects of working in the Civil Service. In your answers to the interview questions, demonstrate that you have what it takes to identify your own development needs and that of others.

MANAGING A QUALITY SERVICE

Whilst working in the Civil Service you will need to provide a fast, efficient and professional service. You must operate effectively, follow strict service guidelines and make sure you strive to continually improve whilst meeting the diverse needs of your customers.

DELIVERING AT PACE

Delivering at pace is about getting things done and completed on time and to a high standard. To work in the Civil Service you will need determination, adaptability, flexibility, enthusiasm and a commitment to very high standards.

Behaviour to Strengths Linking

It is also worth noting that the behaviours also link to the strengths directly, so as well as preparing your behavioural answers you should also prepare strength-based answers related to the role you are applying for.

The following section below shows which strengths are linked to each of the behaviours.

- **Seeing the Bigger Picture:** Challenger, Strategic, Mission and Visionary.
- **Making Effective Decisions:** Analytical, Decisive, Preventer and Problem Solver.
- **Changing and Improving:** Adaptable, Improver, Courageous, Problem Solver, Change Agent and Resilient.
- **Leadership:** Confident, Motivator, Change Agent, Team Leader, Inclusive and Visionary
- **Communicating & Influencing:** Authentic, Inclusive, Emotionally Intelligent, Influencer and Explainer.
- **Working Together:** Challenger, Networker, Emotionally Intelligent, Relationship Builder, Inclusive, Team Player, Negotiator and Mediator.
- **Developing Self and Others:** Enabler, Inclusive, Explainer and Learner.
- **Managing a Quality Service:** Disciplined, Precise, Efficient, Preventer, Focussed, Organiser and Service Focussed.
- **Delivering at Pace:** Adaptable, Organiser, Disciplined, Resilient, Catalyst, Responsible and Focussed.

'Seeing the Bigger Picture' Behavioural Interview Questions

When answering interview questions that are based on seeing the big picture, you must show that you understand exactly how your job position fits into the Civil Service and its goals. You also must show your awareness of how the work you are doing is focused on the wider good of the nation. Try to incorporate in your responses the strengths Challenger, Strategic, Mission and Visionary.

Question 1

Tell me about a time when you had to see the bigger picture?

Sample answer:

I was working in a previous role and my manager came into the office to speak to the team. He explained that, because of the industry changes and trends we were experiencing, and the manner in which people were starting to shift their shopping habits online, we would all need to take on new responsibilities. Some people in the team were not very happy about this, but I encouraged them to view it from a different angle. I explained that, if we all embraced the changes positively, and we looked ahead to the future, we would not only get keep our jobs, but we would help the organization to adapt during these changing times. Eventually, everyone in the team agreed to embrace the new responsibilities that we all had, and the business continued to grow, thrive and develop moving forward.

How is this answer demonstrating 'Seeing the Bigger Picture'?

The big picture is the fact that you were able to see ahead (visionary) in regard to where the company needed to be if it was to survive the inevitable changes to be implemented (strategic). If both you and the other people in the team would have chosen not to embrace the changes, the business would have most probably failed.

Question 2

Describe a situation where you had to work outside of the scope of your usual role?

Sample answer:

I was working as part of a small team in my previous job and a valued and talented member of the team went off sick at short notice. They were going to be off for at least two weeks, and so my manager needed someone in the team to step up and take on their responsibilities. I volunteered to be that person, and I started off by assessing their workload and the skills I would need to quickly develop in order to meet my objectives. I called up the member of staff who was off sick at home to ask them some questions about their work and whether they had any advice they could offer me. I then prioritised which tasks I needed to complete, and how I was going to approach them. By working methodically, and by carrying out some research to find out how to tackle each task competently, I was able to complete all of my work colleagues' tasks and projects to a good standard whilst they were off sick.

How is this answer demonstrating 'Seeing the Bigger Picture'?

The big picture here is the fact that you understood how important it was to go outside of your normal job description to help the organization. Some employees would not do this because they would not see it as their responsibility to cover for someone else. However, if you would have chosen not to volunteer in this situation, the organization would have probably suffered as a result. (strategic & mission).

Question 3

Tell me about a time when you embraced change at work?

Sample answer:

A new manager took over the running of our department and she wanted to make numerous changes that some people in the team felt were unnecessary. However, because we had functioned a set way for a long period of time, I personally felt the changes were a good thing. I listened to my new manager's proposed changes and I offered to help implement them.

She gave me the task of creating new team guidelines that would define the way we would work moving forward. During the transition of change, I actively encouraged other team members to try and embrace the changes positively, and I explained how it would be a positive thing for us all to at least try the new methods of working. Six months after the changes were brought in, the team was performing better than ever, and the vast majority of people team felt the team was in a much stronger position than previously.

How is this answer demonstrating 'Seeing the Bigger Picture'?

Sometimes, seeing the bigger picture is about actively encouraging or helping an organization to change. Most people are not comfortable with change, and the old viewpoint of *"if it isn't broke, why fix it?"* is often heard in some organisations. This is extremely unhelpful to the progression of an organisation, so it is important that you are capable of seeing the bigger picture in respect of how an organization needs to change in order to have a successful future (visionary).

Question 4

Tell me about a time when you went out of your way to help your employer?

Sample answer:

A situation occurred whereby our company website crashed at 3:30pm on a Friday afternoon. This had potentially disastrous connotations because we were due to run an online sale over the weekend that was due to start at 9am on the Saturday morning. I volunteered to stay behind late that evening to help my manager try and find a solution to the problem, and to get the website back up and running in time for the sale on Saturday. I started off by calling around local IT companies but none of them were free to do the work at such short notice. I then used my initiative to find a solution to the problem by using the online outsourcing website UpWork.com. I was able to hire a freelance IT web developer from the website who managed to fix the problem by 6pm that evening. My staying behind late, and by using my initiative, I was able to help the business avert a major problem.

How is this answer demonstrating 'Seeing the Bigger Picture'?

Some people would not help their employer in this type of situation because they may have their own plans that evening, or they may not think it is their responsibility to do so. However, if the organization was unable to run its SALE over the weekend, it would have not only suffered financially, but its brand reputation could have been damaged, too (strategic). By seeing the bigger picture, you understand how important it is to stay behind and help your manager solve this challenging and unforeseen problem (mission).

'Changing and Improving' Behavioural Interview Questions

In your answers to questions that assess your ability to improve and change, you must show that you are capable of coming up with new and creative ways to solve problems and improve your own and your team's performance. You must show the strengths that you are capable of constantly reviewing and improving your performance and periodically asking for, and responding to, feedback from others. Be adaptable, a problem solver and a change agent.

Question 1

Tell me about a time when you initiated change in a team or an organization?

Sample answer:

I was working in a previous department and I had some spare time available one Friday afternoon. I'd had some concerns about the amount of paper and office supplies we were going through, and so I decided to carry out some research online to see if we could save money by ordering from a different supplier and also cutting down on usage. After a few hours conducting research, I managed to find a much cheaper supplier for all of our office supplies, and whilst the minimum order quantities were higher, over the year I calculated we would save in excess of £1,000. I also manged to find an online invoicing system that we could use free of charge. At the time, we had been printing off hundreds of invoices each month and posting them out to our customers, so this was another positive change that would save the company time and money. At the end of that Friday afternoon, I forwarded my proposals to the supervisor who agreed the changes would be a positive change for both the office and the company. A few weeks later, the changes were implemented.

How is this demonstrating 'Changing and Improving'?

You are using your initiative to look for ways to improve and change. You are showing observational and awareness skills to find a way to not only save the company money, but to also help improve the environment by cutting down on the use of paper invoices. This response also highlights the strengths of problem solving and improver.

Question 2

Tell me about a time when you received feedback from someone else and how did you react?

Sample answer:

When I first started working in my previous role, my manager called me into her office a few weeks after starting to give me some constructive feedback. She said that, whilst she was very pleased with my overall performance, she now wanted me to focus on dealing with more customers throughout the day. She went on to explain that she'd noticed I was spending a little too much time making polite conversation with the customers, and whilst it was important to provide great service, I needed to now speed up the process. I immediately took onboard her comments and I went away and analysed my performance. I decided to ask a more experienced work colleague how he approached dealing with customers in order to increase efficiency. He gave me some great tips and pointers for dealing with customers and I successfully implemented these into my daily working practices.

How is this demonstrating 'Changing and Improving'?

You are taking onboard constructive feedback with a positive attitude. You are then going away, analysing your own performance and taking the necessary steps to quickly improve. This shows the strengths of being resilient and a problem solver.

Question 3

Tell me about a time when you had to overcome a setback?

Sample answer:

I was working on a project in a previous role with four other team members. Halfway through the project, one of our parts suppliers unfortunately went into administration. This setback had the potential to put back the project by up to three weeks. The problem was, the client whose project we were working on, had given us a definitive timescale for completion, which could not be put back under any circumstances. We had to find a way to overcome this challenge and so we got together to brainstorm ideas. No other supplier in the immediate area was immediately available. However, I recommended that we widen our search criteria online and eventually we found a supplier who was located internationally. That afternoon, I made contact with the supplier and we began negotiations. Although the parts they were going to supply for the project were going to cost us 10% more than we had budgeted for, it was essential we did not let the client down. Three days later the parts arrived, and we worked around the clock to get the project successfully completed on time and to the right standard.

How is this demonstrating 'Changing and Improving'?

You are changing your approach to a setback in order to overcome the challenge and successfully complete a project as promised. This shows determination, adaptability and resourcefulness.

Question 4

Tell me about a time when you changed the way that you worked?

Sample answer:

In a previous role, I wasn't happy with the way I was carrying out a particular task, and so I decided to ask my manager for guidance. The task in question involved collating departmental sales figures for each quarter which were then presented to company directors who would in turn assess overall company performance. I felt the way I was collating the figures was taking too long, and it wasn't in a visually presentable format. After consulting with my manager, she agreed there was a better way to complete the task.

We both decided a more efficient way would be to use an online app that had the facility to quickly collate the sales figures and then present them in an easy-to-understand presentation that could be accessed by the company directors. After carrying out some research, we agreed the best app to use was called Zoho Analytics. Although the new app cost £36 per month it proved to be very successful and so popular amongst our company directors that they decided to roll it out across the organization.

How is this demonstrating 'Changing and Improving'?

You identified there is a better way of doing things which has significant improvements across the organization. Value for money and efficiency are very important aspects of working in the Civil Service. This also highlights being adaptable, resilience and being a change agent.

'Making Effective Decisions' Behavioural Interview Questions

It is important you use information and data to make accurate decisions whilst working for the Civil Service. This is far more effective than taking unnecessary risks or simply going on gut feeling! When making decisions, show that you consider the options and the likely outcome. The strengths which you will be assessed against will include, Analytical, Decisive, Preventer and Problem Solver.

Question 1

Tell me about a time when you made the right decision?

Sample answer:

I was in a meeting in a previous role discussing a new client project with other team members. Three people within the team proposed that we used a substandard product part for an element of the project in order to save time and money. This type of proposal went against my own personal values of honesty, integrity and professionalism, and so I objected, and I gave my reasons why. I stated that, if we were to take an unnecessary risk of using a substandard product part, not only could this be dangerous, but if the client were to find out, it would irreversibly damage the reputation of the organisation. After putting forward my concerns, everyone agreed we should stick to using the relevant products that met the project specification and criteria.

How Is This Demonstrating Effective Decision Making?

You are demonstrating that you carefully weigh up the risks and the consequences of your decisions and that you put the reputation and the future good of the organization above everything else. By doing this you are showing the strengths of being analytical and preventing issues further down the line during the project.

Question 2

Tell me about a time when you had a difficult challenge?

Sample Answer:

When I first started working in a previous role, I felt it was a challenge to put forward my suggestions and my opinions during meetings. I felt that some of the more senior members of the team were not taking my suggestions and comments seriously, and I wanted to do something about it. I carefully considered my options. I could either blend into the background and keep quiet, or I could say something to try and resolve this difficult situation. Being someone who is enthusiastic and who is keen to contribute, I decided to speak up during one of the meetings. I said that, whilst I could understand and appreciate that my lack of time in the company might be an issue for some people, I genuinely wanted to help the team and I felt I had lots to offer. Just by saying this, it had a profound effect on the way I was treated moving forward. People within my team started to listen to me more and they valued my contributions whenever I put them forward. Whenever I encounter a challenging situation, I will carefully consider my options and I will do things that are in the best interests of the team and the organisation I am a part of.

How Is This Demonstrating Effective Decision Making?

It shows that you carefully weigh up your options before making a decision and it also demonstrates you have the confidence and resilience to overcome challenging situations and solve problems and prevent further issues.

Question 3

Describe a time you came up with an innovative solution to a problem?

Sample answer:

In a previous role, I noticed a significant number of customers were making the same complaint about one of our products. The complaint was based on the fact a large percentage of customers were finding the product difficult to operate once they received it. Nobody within the company had used their initiative to solve the recurring problem. Instead, each customer service call agent was spending at least five minutes explaining to each customer how to use the product once they called in to complain. I decided to use my initiative to make a positive change to this situation. I created clear and concise instructions that could be placed in the box with each product that went out to our customers. I asked a few work colleagues to test the instructions, just to make sure they were clear. Once I had created the instructions, I gave them to my manager for approval. Following the action that I took, customer complaints for this product were totally eradicated.

How Is This Demonstrating Effective Decision Making?

This answer shows that you have the confidence and initiative to solve an ongoing problem (problem solver) that ultimately improves the service that is being provided to customers. Your actions result in a positive outcome for the organization and its customers.

Question 4

Tell me about a time when you had multiple options for solving a difficult problem?

Sample answer:

I was working as part of a team in a previous role and we were tasked with creating a marketing campaign for a new company product launch. We were given a budget to work to and clear instructions that the campaign should deliver a strong return on investment. During the team meeting, everyone put forward lots of different ideas ranging from local newspaper advertising through to online Facebook and Google ads that would be targeted the right audience. This was a difficult decision to make because, as a team, we had so many different options to choose from. I suggested that we should start off by determining the exact goals of the marketing campaign, and then decide which advertising options would be best suited to our goals. By using a logical approach to the task, we agreed that a split of 75:25 in favour of online advertising would be better suited. The reason for this decision was based on the fact we had the option to track the success of the online advertising campaigns as opposed to not having a tracking facility when advertising in the local newspapers. The online advertising campaign proved to be a huge success and soon after launch we decided to shift one hundred percent of the campaign budget over to the online adverts.

How Is This Demonstrating Effective Decision Making?

With this situation you are demonstrating your ability to use a logical and analytical approach to solving difficult problems where you have lots of options available to you. You are also demonstrating your ability to use company finances responsibly, something that is important within the Civil Service.

'Leadership' Behavioural Interview Questions

As a leader within the Civil Service, you must show a passion for delivering excellent public services. You must motivate, inspire and direct others to achieve the objectives of the Civil Service. In everything you do, you must value diversity, you must operate in a fair and respectful manner, and must value and respect other people's contributions whilst creating opportunities for all. You will be assessed on the following strengths also; Confident, Motivator, Change Agent, Team Leader, Inclusive and Visionary.

Question 1

Tell me about a time when you had to lead a team?

Sample answer:

When I first started in my previous role, it was clear that the team I was managing had no direction, they had little motivation and they appeared to lack discipline. It was my responsibility to direct, motivate and inspire the team to achieve the organisations objectives. I started out by briefing the team on my expectations and the standards I expected from everyone. In my opinion, you have to set the bar high as a manager or a leader from the get-go. I then held performance reviews with all members of my team and during these discussions, I assessed each team members strengths, their weaknesses, and their career aspirations. I then provided each person with a development plan of what they needed to do in order to improve and develop over the forthcoming twelve months. Finally, I monitored the team moving forward; I provided them with direction and advice, and I motivated them to achieve the goals I had initially set.

How Is This Demonstrating Leadership?

You are showing that you have the ability to identify weaknesses within a team and you are not afraid to set high standards from the start. This is something that is very important when working in the Civil Service. You then set clear guidelines and you support your team moving forward to achieve the organisations objectives.

This answer demonstrates confidence, being a change agent and motivator.

Question 2

Tell me about a time when you had to deal with a difficult or underperforming employee?

When I first started managing a previous team, I noticed one long-term serving employee was blasé in his approach to tasks. After observing him for a week or so, I decided to speak to him in private. I gave him a number of examples where I felt his performance was not what I would have expected from someone with his experience, and I asked him to explain why. He stated that he'd been working at the organisation for a long time and that his motivation levels had simply diminished over time. I decided to take the necessary action to change this. I gave him an important project to work on, and I set clear guidelines for its completion. I also asked him to be a coach and a support to a new junior member of staff who had recently joined the team. By giving him more responsibility, and by praising him when he completed tasks to a good standard, I was able to quickly improve his motivational levels moving forward.

How Is This Demonstrating Leadership?

Some manager's or team leaders would not have the confidence to deal with this situation due to the experience the team member has. However, you show strong leadership capabilities here because not only do you identify there is a problem early on, you also put clever plans in place to resolve the issue and win over the member of staff.

Question 3

Explain a situation where your style of leadership had a positive impact on a team or a situation?

Sample answer:

In a previous role, I was managing a team who I felt had previously lacked direction and leadership. I utilised a more autocratic style of leadership whereby I set high standards from the very start. I created a set of team values that I expected everyone to adhere to, and I put career progression plans in place for all staff. This had a positive impact on the majority of the team because everyone started to feel valued, appreciated and supported. Although some people did initially push back against my style of leadership, I persevered, and I insisted on high standards. Approximately four months after I started managing the team, we were one of the highest performing units within the company. I put this down to the fact that the style of leadership I used was effective in terms of helping the team to get some structure and discipline, to get some direction and to feel good about the work they were carrying out.

How Is This Demonstrating Leadership?

You are using a style of leadership that is suited to the team you are responsible for. You are putting things in place that will ensure high standards are achieved. Team values and career progression planning are both important aspects of managing and leading a team.

Question 4

Tell me about a time when you had to lead a project?

Sample answer:

I was responsible in a previous role for leading a difficult internal company project that involved different members of the organization. The project brief required me to assess company performance with a view to making recommendations for streamlining operations. I started out by holding a team meeting where I set expectations of what was required by all members of the project team. I defined the scope of the project and asked for people's opinions on how they believed, based on their experiences, we should approach the project. I then set a project action plan and allocated tasks amongst the team. Each team member was given a clear and concise brief and a strict timeline in which to deliver their objectives. Throughout the duration of the project, which lasted for a total of eight weeks, we met frequently as a team, and I measured progress along the way. On two occasions I needed to alter the action plan because I felt it wasn't going to meet the project brief and expectations. Through perseverance, and by using the strengths of each team member, we were able to make excellent recommendations to the company owners for streamlining operations by reallocating key members of staff and using different contractors which all resulted in considerable savings for the organisation.

How Is This Demonstrating Leadership?

To lead a team whilst at the same time managing a difficult project takes skill, determination and resilience. This answer shows that you have the confidence to take control of situations to deliver a project based on a set brief with a strict timeline for completion.

'Communicating and Influencing' Behavioural Interview Questions

Whilst communicating in an organisation such as the Civil Service, you need to use clarity, confidence, purpose and an enthusiastic tone. When communicating with others, show that you are respectful of their views and you take into consideration their needs. To answer these sufficiently, you will need to also display the strengths Authentic, Inclusive, Emotionally Intelligent, Influencer and Explainer in your responses.

Question 1

Tell me about a time when your style of communication resulted in a positive outcome?

Sample answer:

In a previous team, a work colleague of mine was overlooked for a promotion. She was quite upset about it because someone with less experience than her had won the promotion. She was talking about leaving the organisation, which concerned me because I felt this was a gut reaction and she wasn't looking at things with a clear head. So, I sat down and spoke to her to try and persuade her to change her mind, and to see things from a different perspective. I used an empathetic style of communication initially, to show that I understood how she was feeling. I then changed my style to a more positive tone by encouraging her to see how far she had come within the organisation, and that she should try and see the bigger picture in respect of what the organisation needed at this particular time. I went on to explain in a determined tone that her time would come for a promotion in the future, and that the best way to approach this would be to knuckle down, to carry on performing to a high standard and to show her manager that she thoroughly deserved the next one. By using several different styles of communication, I was able to convince my work colleague to look at the situation in a totally different light.

How is this Demonstrating Communicating and Influencing?

In the answer to this question, you are acknowledging the need to use a variety of different communication styles to achieve your objectives. You are also demonstrating an ability to influence someone to see the big picture using effective communication skills.

Question 2

Describe a time when you explained a complex concept to someone else?

Sample answer:

A new member of staff joined our team and I volunteered to teach them how to carry out their daily tasks. Within the company, we used a number of complex software packages that were not easy to understand. I started off by assessing my new work colleagues' level of knowledge before creating a check list of what I needed to teach them. As I progressed through each tutorial, I took my time, I reduced the pace of teaching and I asked them numerous questions to make sure they fully understood each part. I then asked them to try the software package themselves whilst I monitored their performance. On a few occasions, I needed to use simple drawings to explain a particular concept to them. By using drawings that they could relate to, I was able to quickly teach them the elements of the software package that were the hardest to understand. Within five days of starting the process, I managed to get my new work colleague fully up to speed in their role.

How Is This Demonstrating Communicating and Influencing?

Within the answer to this difficult Civil Service interview question, you are being patient, considerate and you are adapting your style of communication to meet the current knowledge level of your work colleague (emotionally intelligent).

Question 3

Explain a situation when you had to communicate a difficult message to someone?

Sample answer:

A relatively new work colleague of mine had inadvertently given wrong information about the availability of an order that a customer was waiting for. The customer had already been let down once before, and so my manager asked me to call them back to give them the news that their long-awaited order would still not be available for another three weeks. Before calling the customer, I considered what I wanted to say, how I was going to say it and how I would deliver this difficult message. I made sure there were no distractions in the room, and I then made the call. I started off by being totally open, honest and upfront with the customer. I apologised unreservedly; I expressed my genuine disappointment for the information they had just received, and I gave them my reassurances their order would be available on a definitive date. The customer was, understandably, very annoyed. I listened to them; I let them vent off and I showed understanding and appreciation for their situation. By using an appropriate style of communication, and by being open and honest, I was able to turn the situation around and keep the customer onboard.

How Is This Demonstrating Communicating and Influencing?

In this type of situation, where you are delivering an understandably disappointing message, you are considering what you are going to do and say beforehand (preplanning) and you are using a style of communication that is suited to the situation. You are also being tactful, and you are taking into account how the customer must be feeling once they receive the news (emotionally intelligent).

Question 4

Tell me about a time when you persuaded someone to see your point of view?

Sample answer:

I was working in an office and another member of staff was about to order some office supplies. She was ordering the minimum quantity required, and I asked her if she felt it might be better to order a larger quantity to save money. She disagreed with me, and she said that she'd prefer to order less because this had a better impact on the environment. I explained to her that, by ordering less we would need to order again in the not too distant future, which would actually be more harmful on the environment, simply because the courier would need to come back time and time again to deliver the goods. By ordering a larger quantity, we would not only be saving money in the long term, because there were discounts to be had, but the courier would only need to do one trip. By explaining to her my thought process in a logical and clear manner, she eventually came around to my way of thinking.

How Is This Demonstrating Communicating and Influencing?

Instead of forcing your view onto the other person, you are taking your time to explain the benefit of your approach (influencer) by using facts and evidence, something that is vital when communicating and influencing.

'Working Together' Behavioural Interview Questions

Within the Civil Service you will need to work alongside other internal members, other departments and external contractors and stakeholders. Therefore, teamwork is an essential skill needed within all roles. In your answers to the 'working together' interview questions, show you have the ability to work with everyone, regardless of their background, views or opinions. In your responses you should include where possible mention of the following strengths; Challenger, Networker, Emotionally Intelligent, Relationship Builder, Inclusive, Team Player, Negotiator and Mediator.

Question 1

Tell me about a time when you worked as part of a team?

Sample answer:

In a previous role, I was asked to be a part of a team whose brief it was to launch a new product for a customer. We got together at the start of the task to nominate a team leader and to discuss the brief and agree a plan of action for moving forward. We all then put forward ideas and suggestions for launching the product based on what we all thought would work best. The team leader then defined the action plan for the product launch, and she allocated tasks to all of us which we needed to complete within a certain timescale. My responsibilities included setting up the online advertising campaigns and talking to local media outlets to try and gain free media coverage. Throughout the project we communicated regularly and clearly, we supported each other with the team tasks, and we focused on achieving our objectives. By working as part of a team, we managed to successfully launch the product for the client who was extremely pleased with the results and the return on investment the launch campaign yielded for them.

How Is This Demonstrating Working Together?

This answer shows you can work effectively as a team player by listening to a brief, by communicating regularly and concisely and by supporting each other (networker, team player) to achieve the objectives. To be effective within a team, you must focus on the end goal, demonstrate adaptability, flexibility and enthusiasm for the task, and be supportive of other team members.

Question 2

Tell me about a time when you had to work with a difficult colleague?

Sample answer:

When I first started work in a previous role, a senior member of the team appeared to take a dislike to me for reasons I did could not understand. This did not really faze me initially, because I was simply focused on doing a good job to a high standard. However, as time went on, I felt the relationship had the potential to impact on our ability to work together in a positive manner, and so I decided to tackle the issue. I asked my work colleague in private if there was anything, I was doing that was either irritating them or causing them to be dismissive. They appeared slightly taken aback by my comments, but I went on to give them a few examples of where the working relationship had not been as harmonious as perhaps it could have been. I went on to explain that I genuinely wanted to do a good job and in order to achieve that goal, I needed to work them in a professional manner, and I also needed to learn from their experience and expertise. By confronting this situation head on it had a positive impact on our working relationship moving forward. From that day on they were far more attentive, supportive and we actually ended up becoming good friends outside of work.

How Is This Demonstrating Working Together?

This answer demonstrates you put the needs of the organisation first. It shows that you do not take things personally, and it also shows that you are a person who is willing to challenge uncomfortable situations with a view to achieving a positive outcome (mediator, relationship builder).

Question 3

What skills have you developed that will help you to work effectively with other people?

Sample answer:

I have gained numerous skills that allow me to be a supportive and productive member of a team. First and foremost, I am a good communicator. I know how important it is to not only speak with clarity and purpose, but to also be a good listener, too. For communication to be effective, it must be a two-way process. I am supportive and encouraging of others, and I will always offer my experience and guidance when needed. Afterall, a good team is only as strong as its weakest member. I am persistent and determined, which means I can motivate others within a team to overcome challenges and problems as and when they occur. I am a fast worker and I will always help people within the team I am a part of to continually improve and develop. Finally, I am someone who is very supportive of change. I believe strongly that, if a team is to perform to a consistently high standard and help the organization to flourish, it must to embrace change in a positive manner.

How Is This Demonstrating Working Together?

This answer provides details of how you approach working as part of a team. It shows that you fully understand which qualities are vital to be a supportive and productive team member. The answer also talks about your understanding of how important change is to the future success of a team and an organization; something that is very important whilst working for the Civil Service.

Question 4

Tell me about a time when you had to deal with conflict in a team?

Sample answer:

In a previous team I was a part of, two work colleagues were constantly bickering and criticizing each other. I believe conflict can be extremely negative to the functioning and performance of a team, so I decided to intervene to try and get the two individuals working in a more harmonious manner. I asked to speak to them both outside in the car park, away from everyone else during a lunch break. I explained to them in a polite manner that the conflict they were both experiencing was affecting the team's performance. I went on to explain that we all had a duty to work together; to put our differences aside and to focus on the team goals. I said to them both, that the rate they were both going with this conflict, their actions would seriously affect the work output of the team, and I wasn't prepared to let this happen. My intervention clearly had a positive impact on both of them, because they agreed to find a way to resolve their differences. By having the confidence to intervene in the conflict, and by explaining the possible outcome of their behaviour, I was able to persuade them both to see the situation in a different light.

How Is This Demonstrating Working Together?

This answer demonstrates you are aware how conflict can impact negatively on a team. It also shows you have the confidence to deal with the situation quickly and it also shows you care about the future performance of your team (relationship builder, mediator).

'Developing Self and Others' Behavioural Interview Questions

Continuous learning and development are vital aspects of working in the Civil Service. In your answers to the interview questions, demonstrate that you have what it takes to identify your own development needs and that of others. Focus also on the following strengths; Enabler, Inclusive, Explainer and Learner.

Question 1

Tell me about a time you helped other people?

Sample answer:

A new member of staff joined our team and her English was not particularly good. I could detect that she was struggling to understand some of the basic principles of her role, and so I decided to help. I introduced myself before offering to support her. Every morning when we started work, I sat down with her for 30 minutes to show her what to do and how to approach each task. I encouraged her along the way and praised her when she completed a task to the required standard. Each day that passed I could see an improvement, and after four weeks she was fully up and running in her role and operating to a high standard. I felt the way in which I helped her during the first few weeks of starting work served to not only increase her confidence, but to also show her that we were a caring and supportive team who she could call upon at any time for help, advice and guidance.

How Is This Demonstrating Developing Self and Others?

This response shows you are someone who identifies quickly when a member of your team is struggling. You are quick to act and everything you do is supportive (explainer, enabler). You are clearly someone who wants to help your work colleagues to learn and grow in a supportive environment.

Question 2

Tell me about a time when you had to deal with underperformance?

Sample answer:

I noticed a work colleague of mine was lacking in motivation and they were making numerous foolish mistakes. They were usually very good at their job, so I knew something wasn't quite right. I am the type of person who understands how, if a member of your team is not performing to the necessary high standards as everyone else, it can have a negative impact on the rest of the team. Therefore, I decided to tackle the situation straight away. I spoke to them during a tea break to ask if everything was okay. They said they were fine, and so I went on to give them a few examples of mistakes they had been making. They then started to open up to me how their partner had recently left them, and they were feeling down and disinterested in work. I showed empathy for their situation, and I talked to them about how they were feeling. I then moved on and I encouraged them to try and be more productive at work as this would help them to feel better about themselves and their unfortunate situation. I mentioned that I had been given a project to work on by our manager, and I suggested they should ask him if they could get involved, too. That way, I could keep a close eye on them and motivate them to do a good job. This proved to be a great move because from that day on, their work performance improved significantly, and they made no more mistakes.

How Is This Demonstrating Developing Self and Others?

This answer demonstrates you fully appreciate how, if underperformance is left unchecked, it can manifest, develop and eventually impact on the wider team and the organisation. Therefore, you are taking immediate steps to help the person improve (enabler). You are also using an appropriate style of communication to deal with the situation, which is extremely important when tackling any form of underperformance.

Question 3

Tell me about a time when you identified a need for self-development or improvement?

Sample answer:

Whilst working in a previous role, I felt my sales techniques were not as good as some of the other members of the team. This concerned me because I did not want to fall behind, and even though I had not been with the company for that long, I was keen to be a high performing member of staff. I carried out a quick self-assessment of my skills and where I needed to improve before putting in place a plan of action to get where I wanted to be. First of all, I signed myself up to an online development course via the website Udemy.com. The course focused on improving sales techniques in the workplace. I paid for this course myself and I studied at home in the evenings. I also asked a work colleague of mine who was particularly good at sales to spend some time showing me the different techniques she used to increase sales. Four weeks after first identifying this training need, I had completed the course and my colleague had provided me with lots of useful tips to implement. A little while later, I became one of the best performing members of the team in respect of sales figures.

How Is This Demonstrating Developing Self and Others?

To have the confidence to identify your own training needs takes honesty and courage. In this response, you are showing that you are passionate about your work and that you have the determination to get where you want to be in the fastest time possible (learner). This level of response will be attractive to any interviewer because it shows you are a self-motivated person.

Question 4

Tell me about a time when you helped a work colleague develop a new skill or improve an existing one?

Sample answer:

I was working in a previous role and a colleague of mine expressed an interest in learning how to do a particular element of my job. They worked in another department, but they needed to gain experience in different areas of the company because they were going for a promotion. I agreed to teach them my role by dedicating one hour each day over a ten-day period. Before I started teaching them, I created a tick sheet of all the things I felt they needed to learn to reach a decent level of competence. I then asked them a few questions to assess their current level of knowledge before methodically working through each area with them. At all times I was patient, I asked them clarifying questions to make sure they fully understood everything along the way, and at the end of the ten-day period, I gave them a short exam to undertake which reaffirmed they had taken everything in that I had taught them. It actually felt quite rewarding to help someone develop a new skill and I feel this something I would like to do more often in the future if the opportunity arises.

How Is This Demonstrating Developing Self and Others?

You are selfless in your actions and you are taking the time to use a structure that ensures your work colleague reaches the correct level of competence for their needs.

Furthermore, you are taking the time to train them over a ten-day period which means they are more likely to retain the information you have passed on to them.

'Managing a Quality Service' Behavioural Interview Questions

Whilst working for the Civil Service you will need to provide a fast, efficient and professional service. You must operate effectively, follow strict service guidelines and make sure you strive to continually improve whilst meeting the diverse needs of your customers. When answering interview questions, please bear in mind the following related strengths: Disciplined, Precise, Efficient, Preventer, Focussed, Organiser and Service Focussed.

Question 1

Can you explain how you would deliver excellent customer service?

Sample answer:

I would make sure my style of communication was tailored to the customer needs and I would be polite, positive and enthusiastic whilst dealing with them. I would be welcoming when they came into contact with the organisation, and I would be professional in all communications. I would ask them question to establish their individual requirements, and I would then respond in a timely manner to ensure I met their specific needs. Whilst dealing with a customer I would always act as a positive role model for the organisation; I would be courteous, and I would make sure I left a lasting, positive impression on them so they felt valued, respected and they wanted to use the service time and time again in the future. Finally, if the opportunity presented itself, I would ask the customer for feedback to try and improve upon the service we had provided them with.

How Is This Demonstrating Managing a Quality Service?

This answer clearly shows you understand what goes to make up a quality service (service focussed). You are following organisational guidelines; (disciplined) you are asking relevant questions and you are being respectful and courteous at all times. You are also showing consideration for the customers' unique and individual needs and you are making sure the contact they have with the organisation is positive. Finally, you are trying to improve the service by asking for feedback.

Question 2

Tell me about a time when you had to manage a quality service?

Sample answer:

In a previous role, it was my responsibility to work with other people in my team to provide excellent customer and client service. Part of our responsibilities included answering customer service telephone calls and we had strict guidelines we all needed to follow. I started out by reading the guidelines carefully to make sure I had the necessary skills needed to do the job to a consistently high standard. Whilst dealing with each customer on the telephone, I would start off with a welcome script and I would then ask them for details relating to their query or their complaint. I would then ask probing questions to get to the bottom of the issue as quickly as possible. At all times whilst on the telephone, I would monitor the time, and I would make sure the needs of the customer were met. If ever I needed to get back to the customer at a later date, I would ensure a reminder was placed on the system so that I never forgot. In my opinion, too many businesses fail to deliver on their promises when getting back to customers and I was keen for this not to happen. At the end of each call with the customer, I would ask them for feedback on the service they had received. This then allowed me to pass on any areas of suggested improvement to my manager, which she then assessed before implementing.

How Is This Demonstrating Managing a Quality Service?

This answer shows you fully understand how to manage and deliver a great service (service focused). You are demonstrating awareness of what customers want and you are trying to continually improve the service by asking for feedback. (focussed) Being able to provide an excellent level of service is paramount to a successful career in the Civil Service.

Question 3

How would you deal with a customer complaint?

Sample answer:

When dealing with a customer complaint I would be totally professional at all times. Remembering that I am representing my employers' brand and their reputation, so I would always be polite, respectful and courteous. I would start off by asking numerous questions to get to the bottom of their complaint. I would use effective listening skills to make the customer feel valued. I would then apologise for the complaint if necessary, and I would put forward a resolution and ask the customer to confirm they were happy with it. I would then take immediate steps to resolve the issue and follow up with the customer to make sure they were still satisfied. Finally, I would assess how the complaint had come about in the first place with a view to trying to prevent the same situation from happening again in the future.

How Is This Demonstrating Managing A Quality Service?

This response provides clear details of the steps you would need to take to resolve any type of complaint. You are being professional, considerate and courteous, and you are making sure you represent the brand in a positive manner. At all times you are focusing on the customer and you are making an effort to ensure the same situation does not happen again in the future (service focussed, preventer).

Question 4

Tell me about a time when you made recommendations that were designed to improve the quality of a service?

Sample answer:

I was working in a previous role and I noticed the same complaint was being made by several customers. Instead of ignoring the issue, or leaving it for someone else to deal with, I decided to investigate further. With permission from my manager, I contacted the customers who made complaints to seek clarification and further information. They all informed me that the issue was with a product we had been selling via our website. The product had unclear and confusing assembly instructions included within the packaging, and these needed to be changed as soon as possible. After I had taken down details of everything the customers had told me, I presented my findings to my manager. We both then investigated the problem and after a few minor tweaks we managed to create amended and clear instructions to accompany the product. From that day forward, we did not receive any further complaints.

How Is This Demonstrating Managing a Quality Service?

You are taking immediate action to respond to an issue that was having a negative impact on the service the company was providing to its customers. This shows that you care about your customers and the service they are receiving (service focussed and preventer).

'Delivering at Pace' Behavioural Interview Questions

Delivering at pace is about getting things done and completed on time and to a high standard. To work in the Civil Service you will need determination, adaptability, flexibility, enthusiasm and a commitment to very high standards. To demonstrate this behaviour, you should focus on the following strengths; Adaptable, Organiser, Disciplined, Resilient, Catalyst, Responsible and Focussed.

Question 1

Tell me about a time when you worked to a strict deadline and what the outcome was?

Sample answer:

I was working on a project in a previous role that had a strict deadline. Part-way through the project the client contacted us to state that he needed numerous changes making to the specification, but that the timeline for completion needed to remain the same. A few people within the team were complaining that it would be too difficult for us to finish the project on time, but I suggested we should still try to complete the project, because the client could become a long-term client of the company. This would obviously be good from a commercial perspective. Following a few team discussions and some major changes to our working schedule, we manged to get the project completed on time, much to the satisfaction of the client. As predicted, the client went on to use our services many times again in the future and I genuinely believe this was as a result of our determination and our willingness to meet their demands.

How Is This Demonstrating Delivering at Pace?

Despite others within your team complaining, you are encouraging everyone to try and complete the project on time, because this will result in a positive outcome for the organisation. This shows adaptability, being organised and being responsible.

Question 2

Tell me about a time when you had to deliver something at pace?

Sample answer:

Late one Monday afternoon, my manager came into the office to ask for a volunteer to complete an urgent time sensitive task. I put my hand up and made myself available to help. My manager then briefed me what I needed to do. The task involved collating six months' worth of company sales figures and putting them into a presentation which he needed to deliver first thing the following morning. I knew I had to work quickly because not only did I need to complete this task on time, I also needed to finish my own work, too. I calculated how much time I had to finish the presentation, and I then set to work. I made sure I had no distractions and I locked myself away in one of the side office rooms so I could maximise the time that I had available. In the end, I decided to stay late after work to complete my own usual tasks because I literally finished the presentation just before 5pm. I believe I am good at working at pace, and I actually enjoy the challenge that comes with working under pressure.

How Is This Demonstrating Delivering at Pace?

This is a great answer to the delivering at pace interview question because it shows you are first to volunteer, (adaptable, responsible) despite not knowing what the task is. It shows you are determined to get things done on time, and it also shows your commitment to your work because you stay behind late that evening to get your own work completed.

Question 3

Tell me about a time when you had to adapt your approach to a task to get it completed?

Sample answer:

Whilst delivering an important presentation at work, the projector broke down. This was a really difficult situation to adapt to, because I had only practised my presentation using PowerPoint and the projector. The easy thing to do would have been to reschedule the presentation, but I knew this would have not been helpful to everyone in the room. I decided to carry on with the presentation by using a different approach. I had a printed copy of my presentation with me, and so I asked a member of the office admin team to quickly print me off some copies which I then handed out to the attendees. I then worked through the presentation whilst referring to the notes, but I used a more engaging style of presentation. To keep the audience engaged I asked more questions, I involved them more in discussions and I asked them lots of questions to clarify their understanding of the subject. By being flexible, adaptable and persistent, I was able to still deliver a fantastic, informative presentation that was very well received by all the attendees.

How Is This Demonstrating Delivering at Pace?

Despite the setback, you displayed a determined and resolute attitude. You remained calm, and refused to choose the easier option, managing to achieve your initial objective, which is to deliver a great presentation on time, and to a high standard (focussed, responsible).

Question 4

Tell me about a time when you completed a project or task having overcome difficult challenges or obstacles along the way?

Sample answer:

In a previous role, I was working on a project for a challenging client who was not only rude, but they were extremely difficult to communicate with. On top of this, I was being let down by contractors who failed to live up to expectations and standards. However, I remained calm and composed, I remained focused on my end goal, and I used adaptability to reach my goal. To overcome the communication issues with the client, I decided to meet with them in person. I tried to establish a common connection with them which helped to defuse any potential conflict. This helped to significantly improve communications moving forward. In respect of the contractors who were letting me down, I decided to use ones from the online website Upwork.com. By using online contractors and freelancers, I was virtually guaranteed to receive a high-quality service that was on time, simply because they knew I had the chance to leave a review based on their performance that other future potential customers would get to see. By remaining calm, and being adaptable and determined in my goals, I was able to overcome the obstacles and deliver the project on time and to a very high standard.

How Is This Demonstrating Delivering at Pace?

Despite the difficulty with the client, you remained

resilient and focussed. You adapted your communication to suit the requirements, and managed to achieve the goal despite the difficulties using organisation skills and being responsible to ensure the project was delivered on time.

Situational Judgement Test

When you apply to join the Civil Service, you will have to complete a number of assessments to assess your suitability to gain employment with the Civil Service.

During the application process, you will be required to sit a number of psychometric tests which will include a situational judgement test. The idea of psychometric tests is to assess candidates on a number of different, assessable, relevant criteria. Psychometric tests do vary in their format and can range from simple numerical and verbal reasoning tests to more complicated job-specific tests.

What is a Situational Judgement Test?

A situational judgement test (SJT) is a form of psychometric test which presents candidates with realistic work-based scenarios, that challenge the candidate to identify the best answer or to order the answers to a set criteria. Situational judgement tests will evaluate your decision-making and allow potential employers to see whether your code of ethics and values match up with theirs. The majority of situational judgement tests do not have right or wrong answers, and simply come down to how an employer assesses the answers of the candidate against their own behavioural/organisational expectations.

The actual test can come in a range of formats such as reading a text passage scenario, watching a video scenario, or even by listening to audio scenarios. The most common types are text-based and video-based.

Choosing Your Answers

The answering process can differ between different situational judgement tests. For example, you may be asked to choose the most effective answer from a multiple choice of options, or you could get asked to rank your answers from a set criteria. This can range from "highly efficient" to "unsuitable" etc. The answer structure will vary between organisations.

A Sample SJT Question & Answer Choice

Please see a typical type of sample situational judgement question to give you a better idea of what to expect.

Sample Question Scenario:

> *You are a senior student in at your local university. One of your tasks is to provide help and advice to any of the first-year students on any issues they may encounter. Over the past year, the university has taken on a number of junior lecturers. One day, a group of first-year students approach you. They are led by a man named Chris:*
>
> **Chris:** *'We're fed up, mate. The training at this university is appalling. I've barely learned anything since I started here.'*
>
> **Greg:** *'Everything about this place stinks. From the way the senior lecturers treat their students, to the bogs on floor two. Low standards.'*
>
> **Kerry:** *'Last week one of the lecturers was watching the football on his phone in the middle of a lecture. It's unacceptable!'*

Take a look at the responses below, and then rank them from most appropriate to least appropriate.

A. *'If you don't like it, there's the door. I'm sure there are plenty of university's who would love to take on a bunch of ungrateful first-year students...'*

B. *'Thank you for letting me know your concerns. If you would like, I can accompany you to the principal's office now, so that we can discuss this further.'*

C. *'I'm sorry to hear that you are unhappy. If it helps, I am happy to offer one-to-one tuition, to get you all get up to speed with things...I charge £30 per hour.'*

D. *'That's terrible to hear. I will bring these issues to the concern of a senior member of staff immediately. Please be assured that we will deal with this as a matter of priority.'*

E. *'Okay, thank you for bringing this to my attention. My advice is to list all of these issues down, and then we can bring it to the attention of a senior member of staff.'*

Which of the responses did you think was the most suitable?

From the suggested most effective to the least effective, please see ranked responses below.

E. *'Okay, thank you for bringing this to my attention. My advice is to list all of these issues down, and then we can bring it to the attention of a senior member of staff.'*

Explanation: This is the best response to the situation. You are assuring the students that this will be dealt with by a senior member of staff, whilst at the same time making sure that when they do approach the senior member of staff they have a comprehensive list of things that need to be discussed.

B. *'Thank you for letting me know your concerns. If you would like, I can accompany you to the principal's office now, so that we can discuss this further.'*

Explanation: This is the second-best option. You are taking very firm and immediate action to deal with the situation. The reason this is the second-best option is that you cannot simply march up to the principal's office with a list of complaints – this needs to be done in an organised fashion. Therefore, it would be better to make an appointment, and get all of the complaints down in a neat list before the meeting.

D. *'That's terrible to hear. I will bring these issues to the concern of a senior member of staff immediately. Please be assured that we will deal with this as a matter of priority.'*

Explanation: This is an acceptable solution, although it's still not ideal. The reason for this is that you haven't taken the time to note down all of their concerns, nor are you involving the principal in the process of dealing with the complaint.

A. *'If you don't like it, there's the door. I'm sure there's plenty of university's who would love to take on a bunch of ungrateful first-year students...'*

Explanation: This is a very bad response. You are completely dismissing their complaints, many of which are serious in nature. This will only harm the university.

C. *'I'm sorry to hear that you are unhappy. If it helps, I am happy to offer one-to-one tuition, to get you all get up to speed with things...I charge £30 per hour.'*

Explanation: This is the worst response. Although you are offering tuition, you are charging them for the time – thereby profiting from the university's ineptitude.

Now you have seen how an example of how a general Situational Judgement Test can be structured, on the following pages we will go into more detail regarding the Civil Service judgement test process.

The Civil Service Judgement Test Process

The Civil Service form of SJT is an online situational judgement test which you will have to undergo as part of your application for any Civil Service role. The purpose of this test is to assess you against a set of competencies called the Civil Service Success Profiles which you will be measured against. The CSJT success profile you are assessed against will be a number of the competencies from the Behaviours section of the Civil Service Success Profiles. These are likely to differ between roles.

In total there are four different variations of SJTs which you could be tested on. This will depend on the vacancy you have applied for, and will include scenarios which are applicable to the behaviours relevant for the role.

An Overview of the Elements of the Civil Service Success Profiles

- **Ability** – Are you able to perform the tasks and be more than competent in the role? This profile focuses on your ability to perform the tasks of the role applied for.

- **Behaviour** – Showing outstanding effective behaviours equates to outstanding performance in the role you are applying for. There are nine different behaviours that you can be assessed against.

- **Experience** – This will be essential especially if you are applying for senior roles within the organisation. You will be expected to be able to demonstrate skills gained though previous roles and not just rely on training once applied.

- **Strengths** – Based on the theory, that if you perform a task on a regular basis and with vigour, this will become a strength. The person will be more prolific and motivated to do a good job.

- **Technical** – With the numerous technical professions available within the government sector, you will need to provide evidence of any technical skills and qualifications gained for certain technical roles. You will also be tested on any knowledge and skills relevant to the role via a number of different tests and assessments.

The Civil Service Judgement Test Structure

There are two different elements to the CSJT, the self-assessment, and the workplace scenario element. The first part focuses on your personality and is very similar to personality questionnaires used in some other job application processes. This provides the assessor with an indication of your ambition level, flexibility, motivation and will provide a basic overview of if you are a good fit for the Civil Service.

It is vital with the self-assessment section you are honest with your answers, as if you pass the initial selection process, you may be asked to elaborate upon these during your interview.

The second part of the CSJT is the workplace scenario section. During this element you will be presented with a number of scenarios which will be relevant to the role including seniority, which you are applying for. The scenarios themselves may be presented to you in either video format or text-based scenarios. The format of the test you will be presented with will depend on the role you are applying for. It's possible that you will have only video, only text or a mixture of both types of scenario formats.

The test itself is not timed and so you can afford to allocate as much time as required for each of the scenarios. When deciding to take the test it is vital that you will be in a comfortable environment where you will not be disturbed by others. Planning the time to do the test is very important, so try to bear in mind the following:

- Find a well-lit and quiet area, where you can sit comfortably to undertake the test using a PC or laptop.

- Allocate a time to do the test, when you are unlikely to be disturbed by others in your household.

- Plan to take the test when you are most mentally active. Do not take the test when you are most fatigued at the end of the day or under the influence of alcohol.

- Ensure you stay hydrated and eat a healthy meal prior to taking your test, this will aid your concentration levels.

- Ensure your internet connection is stable, the last thing you want is to lose your internet connection half way through your test.

- Allocate plenty of time to complete the test, if you think it will take an hour, allocate two hours. Remember the test is not timed, so there is no need to rush.

Taking the Civil Service Judgement Test

If your application is successful, you will receive an invitation to undertake the CSJT and this invitation will also provide full instructions on how to proceed. As we have previously stated, the test is taken online, so there is no need to leave your house to undergo the assessment.

Once you have received your invitation, plan to undertake the test as soon as possible to avoid not missing the deadline for completion.

As previously stated, the first part of the test is the **self-assessment section** which focuses on you as a person and you should answer the questions truthfully as you could be asked to elaborate upon these at your interview. A typical question could be structured as below.

If I see a colleague struggling with a task, I will always offer assistance.

Your task here would be to choose an answer which is an honest evaluation of what you would do. The answer structure will range from Completely Disagree to Completely Agree. Please see choices below.

- Completely Disagree
- Strongly Disagree
- Somewhat Disagree
- Neither Agree or Disagree

- Somewhat Agree
- Strongly Agree
- Completely Agree

Naturally, the Civil Service will be looking for a mark in the strongly or completely agree boxes for this question. The self-assessment part of CSJT accounts for 15% of your overall score.

The second part of the test is the **workplace scenario section**, and this could be presented in either video or text format, or possibly a mixture of both. The idea of the test is for the candidate to read passage of text or watch a short video clip and then rate a number of responses to a set scale.

For each response presented there are four answer choices you can choose from.

- Counterproductive: An unacceptable action that would likely make the situation worse.
- Ineffective: An inept action that would not help the situation.
- Fairly Effective: A suitable action that would be of some benefit to the situation.
- Effective: A worthy action that would assist to resolve the issue.

Do not assume that each response has a different suitability. You may have a scenario, where two of the responses are ineffective. You will also have the opportunity to practice at the start of your test, to familiarise yourself with the format.

Sample Workplace Scenario CSJT Question

You arrive at your desk to find that all of your paperwork for a certain task is missing. You have no idea where it's gone, but you know that a colleague has held a grudge against you ever since you started. What do you do?

1. Confront the colleague and demand that they tell you where they've hidden your paperwork.
2. Remain calm and keep searching for your paperwork around your desk.
3. Speak to your superior and accuse this colleague of hiding your work.
4. Politely ask colleagues, including the one holding a grudge, if they've seen the paperwork that you've misplaced. If this doesn't work, speak to your superior.

Rank the above answer options as either:

- Counterproductive
- Ineffective
- Fairly Effective
- Effective

Please see the suggested answers and explanations for this example scenario below.

Sample Workplace Scenario CSJT Answer

1. Confront the colleague and demand that they tell you where they've hidden your paperwork.

   Answer: Counterproductive

   Explanation: This is an overreaction, and you have no evidence to support your theory that this colleague has stolen your work. You'd also likely be causing a disturbance in the office.

2. Remain calm and keep searching for your paperwork around your desk.

   Answer: Fairly Efficient

   Explanation: This is fairly efficient because you may have just misplaced your work. However, you might also be wasting precious time.

3. Speak to your superior and accuse this colleague of hiding your work.

   Answer: Inefficient

   Explanation: This is better than publicly confronting your colleague and disrupting others but is still inefficient because you have no evidence that they've stolen from you.

4. *Politely ask colleagues, including the one holding a grudge, if they've seen the paperwork that you've misplaced. If this doesn't work, speak to your superior.*

Answer: Efficient

Explanation: This is the best solution as it's possible that someone had to move your paperwork throughout the day. Also, one of your colleagues might have seen the colleague move your paperwork.

All of the questions during this stage of the CSJT will be focused around the Behaviours Success Profile, which has nine different competencies. There will be 3 questions to each of the competencies within the Behaviours profile. The number of competencies you are assessed against will depend on the role you are applying for. The competencies included within the Behaviours Success Profile are:

- Seeing the bigger picture
- Changing and improvement
- Making effective decisions
- Leadership
- Communicating and influencing
- Team working
- Development of self and others

- Managing a quality service
- Delivering at pace

Scoring of the Test and Your Results

Upon completion of the test you will advised of your results, but not if you have passed.

The tests are scored dependent on the number of questions faced and also the difficulty of the test questions faced. Your score will then be compared to other candidates who have taken the same test. When you do receive your results, you will receive these as a percentile. This is not a percentage of questions answered correctly. This is based on your performance compared to the other candidates. For example, if you scored a percentile of 62%, this means that you scored higher than 62% of the other candidates.

All of the roles within the Civil Service are advertised to a certain level. If you have been successful at passing the minimum standard for the level of the role applying for, a number of things may happen. If the role you are applying for requires further tests, you will be sent an invitation to complete the further tests. After the deadline for the test has passed, the assessors will look at all of the candidates scores and will decide upon this what the roles pass mark will be.

After evaluating all results, the assessors can raise the pass mark, but this is generally dependent on the number of candidates amassing the passing score. If the assessors do decide to raise the score, you will be informed of this and if you have passed or not at the raised standard.

Civil Service Situational Judgement Test 1

Read the following 10 scenarios and then rate the effectiveness of each response. For example, if you believe that response 1 is counterproductive, you should place a 1 in the counterproductive box.

Sample Question 1

You are sitting in the staff canteen, when three other members of the team sit down at your table. As you engage in friendly discussion with them, two of the members begin to mock the other person for his religion. Although they are only joking, you can see that the individual in question has been upset by these comments.

1. Join in, it's just a bit of banter.

2. Speak up, and inform your colleagues that they should have more respect for other religions.

3. Ask the offended colleague to speak to you in private afterwards, where you will discuss the comments.

4. Try to change the subject.

Effective	
Fairly Effective	
Ineffective	
Counterproductive	

Sample Question 2

You are sitting in your office. One of your colleagues approaches you. He sits down at your desk and proceeds to inform you that he is a homosexual, and that you are the first person he has told.

Man: 'Please try to keep this a secret, I'm scared of how I'll be treated if other people find out.'

1. Inform your colleague that you have the utmost respect for him, regardless of his sexuality, and that any personal information he shares with you is done so in confidence.

2. Inform your colleague that there is no reason to be ashamed of this, and assure them he will be treated no differently if he shares this with his colleagues.

3. Inform your colleague that there is no place for people like him in the workplace, and that he should hand in his notice.

4. Inform your colleague that his sexuality is nothing be ashamed of, before changing the topic of conversation.

Effective	
Fairly Effective	
Ineffective	
Counterproductive	

Sample Question 3

You are the senior manager at a local council office. One day, one of your staff members knocks on your door. After inviting her in, she tells you the following:

Staff member: 'I'm really sorry, but I've made a mistake. While sorting through my paperwork, I accidentally shredded some of the key reports for the monthly meeting this coming Friday.

1. 'It's okay, we'll just have to proceed without those documents for now. Hopefully they won't be too important.'

2. 'This is a disaster. You've derailed the entire meeting. I'm afraid you're sacked.'

3. 'Okay, don't panic. I'll contact the senior administrator, who should have photocopies of the reports. Later this afternoon though we'll have a serious chat about this.'

4. 'Can you explain to me how this happened? This is a very serious incident.'

Effective	
Fairly Effective	
Ineffective	
Counterproductive	

Sample Question 4

You are working with a colleague, at your local shopping centre conducting a survey for the local council. The two of you are in the middle of your task on the top floor, when you pass by a particular clothing shop. Your colleague gets very excited, dashes into the shop and starts trying on denim jackets.

Colleague: 'I love this shop! I might have to buy a few things from here!'

1. Inform your colleague that they are acting very unprofessionally, and tell them to get back to work.

2. Leave your colleague to it. It's not your problem if they want to mess around.

3. Inform your colleague that you'll be reporting them to your manager for this.

4. Laugh. They are only having a bit of fun.

Effective	
Fairly Effective	
Ineffective	
Counterproductive	

Sample Question 5

You are working at Lionhare council offices. You have a mountain of paperwork to get through, when your senior manager approaches you.

Senior Manager: 'Hey, I need you to fill in this form urgently, it's in regard to the dispute with Mr Hemmingway. Can you get it back to me in the next hour?'

1. 'If you say please.'

2. 'I'll do my best, although I've got a lot of paperwork to complete. Would you prefer me to prioritise this form?'

3. 'No chance, you'll have to wait until tomorrow.'

4. 'Sure, I'll give it immediate priority.'

Effective	
Fairly Effective	
Ineffective	
Counterproductive	

Sample Question 6

It is the start of a new week, and you have been tasked with training a new staff member. Matthew is training to become a surveyor. By the end of your first day, you are very pleased with Matthew's progress, and believe that he will make a great surveyor. Then, your senior manager approaches you:

Senior manager: 'So tomorrow, I'm going to put Matthew with someone else. From what I've seen, he's holding you back and getting in your way. Truth be told, it doesn't seem to me like he's got what it takes.

1. Inform your senior manager that you believe Matthew has great potential, but agree to his working with someone else.

2. Agree with your senior manager. It's her decision, after all.

3. Inform your senior manager that you would like to continue working with Matthew, and that you feel he has strong potential.

4. Ask your senior manager to retract her comments. Inform her that you think she is being unfair and unprofessional.

Effective	
Fairly Effective	
Ineffective	
Counterproductive	

Sample Question 7

You are due to begin your shift with a training candidate, at 9am. Unfortunately, by 5 minutes past 9, he still doesn't seem to have arrived at the office. When you go outside, you find him sleeping in his car.

1. Bang on the window and wake him up. 'You need to start your shift!'

2. Go straight to your manager, and report the candidate. Behaviour like this is not acceptable.

3. Wake the candidate up and then have a serious chat with him. Tell him that unfortunately you will need to report this to your manager.

4. Leave him sleeping. You can handle the shift on your own.

Effective	
Fairly Effective	
Ineffective	
Counterproductive	

Sample Question 8

You are working on the reception desk at Lionhare council offices, when a woman comes in through the door. She appears to be fairly distressed:

Woman: 'No...speak bad English. I don't understand. Please, help.'

1. Tell the woman that you cannot help her if she is unable to explain herself properly.

2. Ask the woman to take a seat and you will contact someone who can assist her.

3. Ask the woman if she could talk a little louder.

4. Try to calm the woman down, before speaking to her slowly and clearly, and trying to establish clues from her language.

Effective	
Fairly Effective	
Ineffective	
Counterproductive	

Sample Question 9

You are working with a trainee. At the end of the day, as you sort through paperwork, you notice that the trainee has made a big mistake. Unfortunately, he has already gone home.

1. Correct his mistake and pretend it never happened. You haven't got time for him to amend it himself.

2. Highlight the error, in pencil, and then leave the paperwork on his desk, for the next morning. He needs to learn from his mistakes.

3. Correct his mistake but sit down with him in the next morning to talk about the error.

4. Call him on his mobile to let him know about his error. Inform him that you are extremely disappointed.

Effective	
Fairly Effective	
Ineffective	
Counterproductive	

Sample Question 10

You are the manager of a local council facility. The previous day, one of your staff members was using a ladder to retrieve an item from storage. Due to incorrect safety precautions, the ladder fell, injuring the staff member. She has broken her ankle, and therefore won't be in work for a significant period of time. It is your job to call her the next day. What do you say to her?

1. 'Hi. I'm really sorry about the incident that occurred yesterday. We hope to see you back at work soon.'

2. 'Hi. Unfortunately, since you are part time, and can no longer work, we are going to have to terminate your contract.'

3. 'Hi. Do you think you could come in and work on crutches?'

4. 'Hi. I'm really sorry about the incident that took place at work yesterday. I'd like to assure you that we will conduct a full investigation of the incident, to ensure it doesn't happen again.'

Effective	
Fairly Effective	
Ineffective	
Counterproductive	

Answers

Question 1 Answers:

1. 'Join in, it's just a bit of banter.'

Answer: Counterproductive

Explanation: This is a counterproductive response. Religion is not something that should be mocked, and you can clearly see that the individual in question has taken the remarks badly.

2. 'Speak up, and inform your colleagues that they should have more respect for other religions.'

Answer: Effective

Explanation: This is an efficient response, as you are clearly demonstrating to the affected individual that discrimination of any kind will not be tolerated, as well as admonishing your colleagues for their behaviour.

3. 'Ask the offended colleague to speak to you in private afterwards, where you will discuss the comments.'

Answer: Fairly Effective

Explanation: This response is fairly efficient. You are showing your colleague that discrimination is not acceptable, but at the same time you are not demonstrating this to the individuals who have upset him.

4. 'Try to change the subject.'

Answer: Ineffective

Explanation: This is an inefficient response. You need to make sure that the problem is addressed.

Question 2 Answers:

1. Inform your colleague that you have the utmost respect for him, regardless of his sexuality, and that any personal information he shares with you is done so in confidence.

Answer: Effective

Explanation: This is effective because you are showing your colleague respect/demonstrating equality, and assuring him that the information will remain confidential as per his request.

2. Inform your colleague that there is no reason to be ashamed of this, and assure them he will be treated no differently if he shares this with his colleagues.

Answer: Fairly Effective.

Explanation: This answer is fairly effective because you are supporting your colleague and reassuring him that his sexuality will have no bearing on how he is treated. However, it's important to consider that he has asked for the information to remain confidential which is not addressed in this response.

3. Inform your colleague that there is no place for people like him in the workplace, and that he should hand in his notice.

Answer: Counterproductive

Explanation: This is counterproductive because you are showing extreme intolerance, and making the individual feel unwelcome.

4. Inform your colleague that his sexuality is nothing be ashamed of, before changing the topic of conversation.

Answer: Ineffective.

Explanation: This is ineffective because even though you are assuring your colleague of your confidentiality, changing the conversation is dismissing the colleague and preventing him from discussing any further.

Question 3 Answers:

1. 'It's okay, we'll just have to proceed without those documents for now. Hopefully they won't be too important.'

Answer: Ineffective

Explanation: This answer is ineffective because the documents are important, and that it's likely you will need them later down the line. In this answer, you are simply ignoring the problem.

2. 'This is a disaster. You've derailed the entire meeting. I'm afraid you're sacked.'

Answer: Counterproductive

Explanation: This is counterproductive because you are taking extremely rash and unnecessary action. Furthermore, based on the role that this question gives you (senior manager) there is no indication that you have the power to remove people from their job.

3. 'Okay, don't panic. I'll contact the senior administrator, who should have photocopies of the reports. Later this afternoon though we'll have a serious chat about this.'

Answer: Effective

Explanation: This response is effective because you are offering a solution to the problem, calming the individual down, and informing them that there could be repercussions for their mistake.

4. 'Can you explain to me how this happened? This is a very serious incident.'

Answer: Fairly Effective.

Explanation: This response is fairly effective because you are taking a serious approach to the problem, and identifying to the individual that it needs to be dealt with.

Question 4 Answers:

1. Inform your colleague that they are acting very unprofessionally, and tell them to get back to work.

Answer: Effective

Explanation: This is the most effective response. You are clearly indicating to your colleague that they are not acting in an acceptable manner, and are encouraging them to focus on the job at hand.

2. Leave your colleague to it. It's not your problem if they want to mess around.

Answer: Ineffective

Explanation: This is ineffective as you are simply ignoring the issue.

3. Inform your colleague that you'll be reporting them to your manager for this.

Answer: Fairly Effective

Explanation: This is fairly effective, albeit perhaps a little unnecessary. In this instance, your colleague's unprofessional behaviour could be dealt with by giving them a stern warning, rather than immediately escalating the matter further.

4. Laugh. They are only having a bit of fun.

Answer: Counterproductive.

Explanation: This is counterproductive. By laughing, you are encouraging their behaviour.

Question 5 Answers:

1. 'If you say please.'

Answer: Counterproductive

Explanation: This is rude/disrespectful to your superior.

2. 'I'll do my best, although I've got a lot of paperwork to complete. Would you prefer me to prioritise this form?'

Answer: Effective

Explanation: This is effective as you are assuring the manager that you will aim to complete the task, whilst also providing an explanation for why it may be difficult.

3. 'No chance, you'll have to wait until tomorrow.'

Answer: Ineffective

Explanation: Not only is this quite rude, but you are giving no attempt or effort to try and get the work completed, nor are you even providing an explanation.

4. 'Sure, I'll give it immediate priority.'

Answer: Fairly Effective

Explanation: This is a fairly effective response, although it does not take into account the other work that you need to do.

Question 6 Answers:

1. Inform your senior manager that you believe Matthew has great potential, but agree to his working with someone else.

Answer: Fairly Effective

Explanation: This is a fairly effective response. You are clearly correcting the manager on his judgement of Matthew, but at the same time are reaching a compromise/not going against his instructions.

2. Agree with your senior manager. It's her decision, after all.

Answer: Ineffective

Explanation: This is an ineffective response. You are ignoring your own judgement of the situation, and letting the senior officer maintain an opinion that is (in your view) incorrect.

3. Inform your senior manager that you would like to continue working with Matthew, and that you feel he has strong potential.

Answer: Effective

Explanation: This is an effective response. The question clearly indicates that you are pleased with Matthew's progress. Therefore, this is what you should tell your senior manager.

4. Ask your senior manager to retract her comments. Inform her that you think she is being unfair and unprofessional.

Answer: Counterproductive

Explanation: This is a big overreaction. It's entirely possible that your senior manager has simply made a mistake, which you can easily correct her on, without being insulting.

Question 7 Answers:

1. Bang on the window and wake him up. "You need to start your shift!"

Answer: Ineffective.

Explanation: It's not enough to just wake the trainee up, you need to try and understand his behaviour, and then report it.

2. Go straight to your manager, and report the trainee. Behaviour like this is not acceptable.

Answer: Fairly Effective

Explanation: This is a fairly effective response to the scenario. However, the best response would be to talk with the beforehand, to try and understand his behaviour.

3. Wake the candidate up and then have a serious chat with him. Tell him that unfortunately you will need to report this to your manager.

Answer: Effective

Explanation: This is the most effective response to this scenario. Although you could go straight to your manager, it is best to wake the trainee officer first, to explain to him the seriousness of the situation.

4. Leave him sleeping. You can handle the shift on your own.

Answer: Counterproductive

Explanation: You should not be expected to deal with a shift on your own, simply because your trainee has overslept/is late for work. This is counterproductive.

Question 8 Answers:

1. Tell the woman that you cannot help her if she is unable to explain herself properly.

Answer: Counterproductive

Explanation: This is extremely unhelpful and contrary to your role. You will only make the woman more upset.

2. Ask the woman to take a seat and you will contact someone who can assist her.

Answer: Fairly Effective

Explanation: This is a fairly effective response as you are still providing the woman with adequate assistance. That being said, you should do your utmost to try and understand the woman's issue, before you contact someone else to assist her.

3. Ask the woman if she could talk a little louder.

Answer: Ineffective

Explanation: This is an ineffective response. The problem is not that the woman is talking too quietly, but with the language barrier.

4. Try to calm the woman down, before speaking to her slowly and clearly, and trying to establish clues from her language.

Answer: Effective

Explanation: This is the most effective response to the scenario. You are making a sustained effort to understand the woman's issue yourself, before moving this to someone with more authority.

Question 9 Answers:

1. Correct his mistake and pretend it never happened. You haven't got time for him to amend it himself.

Answer: Ineffective.

Explanation: This is an ineffective response because you are not giving the trainee any indication that he made a mistake, and therefore he will fail to learn from this.

2. Highlight the error in, pencil, and then leave the paperwork on his desk, for the next morning. He needs to learn from his mistakes.

Answer: Fairly Effective.

Explanation: You are giving the trainee a chance to learn from his mistake, although it be better to actually talk with him about the error.

3. Correct his mistake but sit down with him in the next morning to talk about the error.

Answer: Effective.

Explanation: This is the most effective response to the scenario. You are ensuring that the paperwork gets in on time, whilst still alerting the trainee of their error.

4. Call him on his mobile to let him know about his error. Inform him that you are extremely disappointed.

Answer: Counterproductive

Explanation: This is not productive. You are going out of your way to scold the trainee, and offering him no constructive feedback.

Question 10 Answers:

1. 'Hi. I'm really sorry about the incident that occurred yesterday. We hope to see you back at work soon.'

Answer: Fairly Effective

Explanation: This is fairly effective, because it shows a willingness to take responsibility for the incident and a level of care for the employee. However, you have failed to make reassurances that the incident is being looked into.

2. 'Hi. Unfortunately, since you are part time, and can no longer work, we are going to have to terminate your contract.'

Answer: Counterproductive

Explanation: This is counterproductive. It shows a lack of care and professionalism, and is completely unfair on the employee, particularly since it was the company's fault to begin with.

3. 'Hi. Do you think you could come in and work on crutches?'

Answer: Inefficient

Explanation: This is inefficient. The employee is obviously unable to continue working on crutches and therefore would not benefit them or the company.

4. 'Hi. I'm really sorry about the incident that took place at work yesterday. I'd like to assure you that we will conduct a full investigation of the incident, to ensure it doesn't happen again.'

Answer: Effective

Explanation: This is an effective response to the situation. You are making clear reassurances that the problem will be looked into, and apologising to the employee.

Civil Service Situational Judgement Test 2

Read the following scenarios and then rate the effectiveness of each response. For example, if you believe that response 1 is counterproductive, you should place a 1 in the counterproductive box.

You have 20 minutes to complete the 15 questions.

Civil Service Situational Judgement Test 2

QUESTION 1

You are working in an office when a member of staff, who is in a wheelchair, approaches you. She asks you if you would be willing to swap desks, as your desk is closer to the supplies cupboard, and she finds it difficult to carry lots of supplies back to her desk. How do you react?

1. Say no. You are already settled in at your desk and to move would cause unnecessary upheaval.

2. Say yes. This is not a problem for you and you can see why moving desks would help her out and improve her working day.

3. Tell her to speak to your boss first, to see if he is in agreement with her request. If he doesn't have a problem with it, neither do you.

4. Tell her you would be willing to swap desks providing she is prepared to move all of your belongings to the new desk.

Effective	
Fairly Effective	
Ineffective	
Counterproductive	

QUESTION 2

You are a staff member at a council facility. You recently took a week off for a relative's funeral. Upon your return to work, you hear that your manager has been gossiping about you behind your back, with the other staff at your work. According to your source, your manager questioned the necessity of taking 5 days off for a funeral, and called you lazy. You are upset by these claims. What do you do?

1. Spread bad rumours about your manager. Two can play that game.

2. Take your manager to one side and question her on whether the claims are true. Explain why you needed the time off.

3. Arrange a team meeting to try and get to the bottom of this.

4. Ring your manager in your own time to try and discuss the situation further.

Effective	
Fairly Effective	
Ineffective	
Counterproductive	

QUESTION 3

You are working as a Health and Safety assessor and are visiting a local warehouse to talk to the staff about risk assessments. Whilst walking around the warehouse you notice that a number of the fire doors are wedged open illegally. What do you do?

1. Ignore it. You are at the premise to talk to the staff about a specific subject and it would be inappropriate to say anything there and then.

2. Remove the wedges yourself and then report the situation to the local Fire Safety Officer when you return to your office later that day. He/she can then carry out a formal inspection.

3. Inform the responsible person at the warehouse that the wedges need to be moved immediately. Then, once you return to the office you will report the matter to your local Fire Safety Officer so that he/she can carry out a thorough inspection of the premise.

4. Remove the wedges holding the doors open yourself and say nothing more about it.

Effective	
Fairly Effective	
Ineffective	
Counterproductive	

QUESTION 4

During an office meeting your manager is explaining a number of changes that are being introduced to the working day. These changes will mean that you and your work colleagues will have more tasks to complete during the working day. The majority of other members of the team start to make their objections to the changes heard. What would you do?

1. Join in with the objections. Why change things when everything is going OK as it is?

2. Keep your head down. Whilst you don't agree with the changes you don't want to get into trouble for raising your concerns.

3. Accept the changes yourself. It doesn't matter what the others think. After all, they are entitled to their own opinion.

4. Accept the changes. Change is part of working life. You would also try and explain the benefit of the changes to those who are sceptical.

Effective	
Fairly Effective	
Ineffective	
Counterproductive	

QUESTION 5

> You are managing a team at a distribution centre. It is approaching the annual peak time for business where your staff will need to be at their best in order to cope with demand. You are concerned as staff have been making careless mistakes whilst dispatching goods, due to increased workload. What would you do?
>
> 1. Get the team together and tell them that, if matters do not improve, you will speak to the main boss about getting them replaced.
>
> 2. Hold a team meeting as soon as possible to establish the reasons why so many mistakes are being made. Then, formulate and agree a plan with all of the team in order to improve performance.
>
> 3. Get stuck in yourself more to help the team out. Clearly, they are very busy and they could do with an extra pair of hands.
>
> 4. Speak to your boss and explain to her that you need to take on another member of staff to ease the pressure on the team.

Effective	
Fairly Effective	
Ineffective	
Counterproductive	

QUESTION 6

You are a supervisor working for a council establishment. You are in a meeting with your manager along with ten other supervisors. Your manager has a very strong accent different to your own and tends to talk quickly, often making it difficult for people to understand her. So far, during the meeting, you have not been able to understand most of what she has been saying. What would you do?

1. As soon as there becomes a natural break in her talk, raise your hand and explain that you are finding it difficult to understand most of what she is saying. Respectfully ask if she would please slow down so that you can take in all of the important information she is relaying.

2. Wait to the end of the meeting and then ask your work colleagues for clarification on what she was saying.

3. Wait to the end of the meeting before speaking to her in private and explain to her that you didn't understand most of what she was saying.

4. Do nothing.

Effective	
Fairly Effective	
Ineffective	
Counterproductive	

QUESTION 7

You are a supervisor for a small council service and you have been carrying out interviews for a new role within the company. You interviewed 4 people for the new role and one of them has been successful. After you write rejection letters to the 3 candidates who were unsuccessful, one of them arrives at your office to complain. He says he is bitterly disappointed in the fact he was not successful and wants an explanation from you. What would you do?

1. Tell him you are not obliged to go into reasons why he was not successful, and ask him to leave.

2. Provide him with a short list of reasons for why he was unsuccessful, and encourage him to apply for future positions.

3. Listen to his concerns and allow him to vent his frustrations. Once he has finished, explain to him that there is a robust and thorough selection process in place and that unfortunately, on this occasion, he was unsuccessful and that someone else was found more suitable for the role. Then, offer him constructive feedback on his performance during the interview.

4. Invite him to sit down and make him a cup of tea. Whilst you are out of the office, call your boss and ask for advice on how to deal with the situation.

Effective	
Fairly Effective	
Ineffective	
Counterproductive	

QUESTION 8

You have just started a new job as a manager with a large corporate company. On your first day at work another manager approaches you and starts telling you negative things about your boss. She tells you that he is very poor at doing his job and that you shouldn't trust him as he tends to speak about his staff behind their backs. What would you do?

1. Challenge her in a respectable manner and say that you think she is wrong for saying these things about a senior member of the team.

2. Thank her for the information and be on your guard from now on when dealing with your manager.

3. Thank her for the information but explain that you do not want to pre-judge people and you want to have an entirely open mind. You will take him as you find him.

4. Thank her for the information and then ask other people within the organisation if they have had the same experience whilst working with your manager.

Effective	
Fairly Effective	
Ineffective	
Counterproductive	

QUESTION 9

You are working as an admin assistant in a typical office environment when you can't help overhearing your manager reprimanding one of your work colleagues for poor performance. Your manager is clearly not happy with your colleague and he is making it perfectly clear that he expects to see rapid improvement. You are concerned for your work colleague as he hasn't been himself lately, and you can see that something has been troubling him. What would you do?

1. Speak to your colleague in private and ask him whether anything is wrong. You would offer your support to see if you can help him through this difficult period he is going through.

2. Approach your manager in confidence and tell him that you think there might be something wrong with your work colleague, which is ultimately having an impact on his work performance.

3. Do nothing. You do not want to interfere as it is not your problem.

4. Speak to your work colleague and offer to do some of his work for him in order to ease the pressure he is under from his manager.

Effective	
Fairly Effective	
Ineffective	
Counterproductive	

QUESTION 10

You have been working in a new team for 3 months now. When you started, your line manager put you on a 6-month development programme where you would be closely supervised for that period of time. You now feel very much ready to work alone and the close supervision is starting to frustrate you and hinder your development. What would you do?

1. Complete the 6-month supervision period as planned and don't say anything about how you feel.

2. Tell your work colleagues how you feel and get their advice on what they think you should do.

3. Start working more on your own without telling anyone.

4. Arrange a meeting with your line manager to explain how you now feel ready to work more on your own, unsupervised. Ask for his permission for the supervision period to come to an end.

Effective	
Fairly Effective	
Ineffective	
Counterproductive	

QUESTION 11

You are the project manager of a team of 5. Your group has been tasked with analysing and correlating key intelligence information which has been passed on to you by another sector, before sending it off to management. Halfway through the project, one of your team members approaches you, claiming that she no longer wants to work with another member of the team. The reason for this is that she believes the person in question has been undermining her and making sarcastic comments directed at her. You have not heard anything of this sort. The individual threatening to leave the team is highly experienced and her absence would severely damage the group's chances of success. What would you do?

1. Explain to your team member that the group needs her, and that she should rise above it and continue with the project.

2. Wait to see if you hear anything as mentioned by the individual, and then take action.

3. Sit the individual in question down, and ask their side of the story.

4. Sit them both down to try and resolve the issue, before continuing on with the project.

Effective	
Fairly Effective	
Ineffective	
Counterproductive	

QUESTION 12

> You are a supervisor working in a warehouse and it is 30 minutes until your shift ends. The oncoming shift supervisor calls you and tells you he is going to be 30 minutes late as he is stuck in traffic. You have a dinner date booked with your girlfriend that evening and you need to get away. What would you do?
>
> 1. Tell the oncoming shift workers that they will have to work on their own, unsupervised, for 30 minutes until their supervisor arrives.
>
> 2. Call your girlfriend and tell her you will be late coming home. Then, supervise the oncoming shift workers until their supervisor arrives.
>
> 3. Call your boss and ask her what she thinks you should do.
>
> 4. Just leave at the end of your shift. The fact that he is going to be late is not your problem.

Effective	
Fairly Effective	
Ineffective	
Counterproductive	

QUESTION 13

> You are a manager of a council run local depot and you receive a call from your area manager at head office. She has requested that you spend the day managing at another council service twenty-five miles away as the current manager there has gone off sick. You have a large amount of paperwork to catch up on and you intended on doing it today whilst working at your own office. What would you do?
>
> 1. Explain that you cannot meet their request as you have lots of paperwork work to catch up on.
>
> 2. Explain to head office that you have lots of paperwork to catch up on and ask them how they want you to prioritise your work.
>
> 3. Tell head office that you have lots of paperwork to catch up on but that you are prepared to ring around the other depots in the region to see if there is another manager available to go to the depot. If not, then you would be prepared to go and you would have to catch up with your paperwork another time.
>
> 4. Agree to go to the depot for the rest of the day and take your paperwork with you to do, whilst you are there.

Effective	
Fairly Effective	
Ineffective	
Counterproductive	

QUESTION 14

You are working as a retail shop assistant and it is your turn to work on the customer services desk. A man, who appears to be angry, approaches you with an electric shaver in his hand. He tells you that he only bought the shaver from your shop three weeks ago but that it has now stopped working completely. He wants a replacement to be provided. The shop has a 28-day refund/exchange policy providing a receipt can be supplied. He does not have a receipt. What would you do?

1. Apologise for the inconvenience that has been caused through the defective shaver. Explain to the customer the company's refund policy and that a receipt is required for a refund or exchange. However, explain to him that, if he can provide proof of purchase, by way of a card statement, that you will ask your manager if you can exchange the shaver for him.

2. Explain to him that, because he does not have a receipt, you are not able to help him.

3. Apologise for the inconvenience that has been caused through the defective shaver and then happily exchange the defective shaver for a new one.

4. Ask your manager what he thinks you should do.

Effective	
Fairly Effective	
Ineffective	
Counterproductive	

QUESTION 15

You are a supervisor in charge of completing an important presentation that is being presented this afternoon. You show it to your boss and ask for their feedback. Whilst he says he is impressed with the overall layout and design of the presentation; he has a few concerns. He feels as though the presentation is lacking in statistics and financial data, which is crucial to this presentation's success. You know that adding this information is going to take time, and you are not sure if you have enough research to go on to add this information in such short notice. What would you do?

1. Explain to your boss that the presentation is being presented that afternoon, and ask him for ideas on how to implement this information in time.

2. Inform your boss that whilst you cannot add in this information due to time constraints, you will be happy to answer any questions they have.

3. Ignore your boss's concerns and present the presentation the way it is.

4. Ask your colleagues to help you with the additional information, so that you can ensure the work gets added.

Effective	
Fairly Effective	
Ineffective	
Counterproductive	

SUGGESTED ANSWERS AND EXPLANATIONS
QUESTION 1

1. Say no. You are already settled in at your desk and to move would cause unnecessary upheaval.

Answer: Counterproductive

Explanation: This is counterproductive. The lady is disabled and by not agreeing to her request you are failing to help improve her working environment. By choosing this option you will also serve to deteriorate your working relationship with both her and the rest of your team.

2. Say yes. This is not a problem for you and you can see why moving desks would help her out and improve her working day.

Answer: Effective

Explanation: This is effective. Not only does it improve her working environment, it also serves to improve/enhance relations within the office environment.

3. Tell her to speak to your boss first, to see if he is in agreement with her request. If he doesn't have a problem with it, neither do you.

Answer: Fairly Effective

Explanation: This is fairly effective, simply because you are informing your boss what the proposed plan is regarding swapping desks.

4. Tell her you would be willing to swap desks providing she is prepared to move all of your belongings to the new desk.

Answer: Ineffective

Explanation: This is ineffective. Although you have agreed to the desk swap, the lady is in a wheelchair has already expressed that she finds it difficult to carry lots of items at once so may be unable to move your belongings.

QUESTION 2

1. Spread bad rumours about your manager. Two can play that game.

Answer: Counterproductive

Explanation: This is counterproductive. It is extremely unprofessional, and could only lead to more trouble. You should be the better person.

2. Take your manager to one side and question her on whether the claims are true. Explain why you needed the time off.

Answer: Effective

Explanation: This is effective, as it constitutes the most reasonable

response. It shows both professionalism and integrity.

3. Arrange a team meeting to try to get to the bottom of this.

Answer: Ineffective

Explanation: This is an ineffective response, as you are involving your colleagues in a situation between you and your manager. You should be aiming to stop them gossiping or getting involved, therefore conducting a meeting will only make the situation worse.

4. Ring your manager in your own time to try and discuss the situation further.

Answer: Fairly Effective

Explanation: This is a fairly effective response, as it shows that you are looking to try and resolve the situation in a positive manner.

QUESTION 3

1. Ignore it. You are at the premise to talk to the staff about a specific subject and it would be inappropriate to say anything there and then.

Answer: Counterproductive

Civil Service Situational Judgement Test 2

Explanation: This is counterproductive. As a Health and Safety assessor, you have a responsibility to take action.

2. Remove the wedges yourself and then report the situation to the local Fire Safety Officer when you return to your office later that day. He/she can then carry out a formal inspection.

Answer: Fairly Effective

Explanation: This is a fairly effective response. Not only are you making the premise safer by removing the wedges whilst you are there, making the premise safer in the process, but you are also informing the Fire Service so they can carry out a thorough inspection of the premise.

3. Inform the responsible person at the warehouse that the wedges need to be moved immediately. Then, once you return to the office you will report the matter to your local Fire Safety Officer so that he/she can carry out a thorough inspection of the premise.

Answer: Effective

Explanation: This is effective. Not only are you asking the responsible person to remove the wedges straight away, which educates them and makes the premise safer, you are also informing the Fire Service so they can carry out a thorough inspection of the premise.

4. Remove the wedges holding the doors open yourself and say nothing more about it the concern.

Answer: Ineffective

Explanation: Whilst you are making the premise safer by removing the wedges yourself, it is likely they will be put back soon after. You need to discuss this with someone.

QUESTION 4

1. Join in with the objections. Why change things when everything is going OK as it is?

Answer: Counterproductive

Explanation: Not only are you objecting to the change just because everyone else is, you are also not being open to the opportunities that can be brought to the organisation. For an organisation to grow and develop, change is inevitable.

2. Keep your head down. Whilst you don't agree with the changes you don't want to get into trouble for raising your concerns.

Answer: Ineffective

Explanation: This isn't particularly effective. You are 'sort of' accepting the changes, despite disagreeing with them. In order for changes to be successful in any organisation, everyone must believe in them.

3. Accept the changes yourself. It doesn't matter what the others think. After all, they are entitled to their own opinion.

Answer: Fairly Effective

Explanation: This is a fairly effective response. Whilst you are not going the extra mile to educate your work colleagues on the benefit of change, you are accepting of them.

4. Accept and embrace the changes. Change is part of working life. You would also try and explain the benefit of the changes to those who are sceptical.

Answer: Effective

Explanation: Not only are you embracing and accepting the changes, but you are also going out of your way to explain the benefit to others, which in turn improves the efficiency of the organisation.

QUESTION 5

1. Get the team together and tell them that, if matters do not improve, you will speak to the main boss about getting them replaced.

Answer: Counterproductive

Explanation: This is counterproductive. Not only could this have a negative impact on team morale, you are also failing to establish why the mistakes are being made in the first place. If you dismiss the team and replace them with new staff, the same mistakes might not go away.

2. Hold a team meeting as soon as possible to establish the reasons why so many mistakes are being made. Then, formulate and agree a plan with all of the team in order to improve performance.

Answer: Effective

Explanation: This is effective, as you are communicating with the team to establish why the mistakes are being made. This will enable you to create a plan to improve performance that everyone can follow.

3. Get stuck in yourself more to help the team out. Clearly they are very busy and they could do with an extra pair of hands.

Answer: Fairly Effective

Explanation: This is fairly effective. If the mistakes are being made due to increased workload, it will benefit yourself and the team for you to tackle the increased workload together.

4. Speak to your boss and explain to her that you need to take on another member of staff to ease the pressure on the team.

Answer: Ineffective

Explanation: This is ineffective, because the team will see that there are no repercussions for the errors they have been making and that by not completing their tasks correctly someone else will be bought in to pick up the slack.

QUESTION 6

1. Tell him you are not obliged to go into reasons why he was not successful, and ask him to leave.

Answer: Counterproductive

Explanation: This is a counterproductive response. Whilst you are correct in the fact that you are not obliged to go into the reasons why he was unsuccessful, this does not present your company in a positive light. It would just serve to make the situation worse.

2. Provide him with a short list of reasons for why he was unsuccessful, and encourage him to apply for future positions.

Answer: Fairly Effective

Explanation: This is a fairly effective response. You are potentially leading him along and giving him false hope. He will, quite rightly, expect to be successful at any future interviews he attends. This option just places you in a difficult position.

3. Listen to his concerns and allow him to vent his frustrations. Once he has finished, explain to him that there is a robust and thorough selection process in place and that unfortunately, on this occasion, he was unsuccessful and that someone else was found more suitable for the role. Then, offer him constructive feedback on his performance during the interview.

Answer: Effective

Explanation: This is an effective response. You are allowing him to get his frustrations off his chest, and you are giving him a valid reason for why he was unsuccessful. You are then offering him feedback on his performance so that he can improve for any future interviews he might attend.

4. Invite him to sit down and make him a cup of tea. Whilst you are out of the office, call your boss and ask for advice on how to deal with the situation.

Answer: Ineffective

Explanation: This is an inefficient response. Although you are seeking advice on what to do next from your manager, you are not taking the lead and using your initiative to deal with the situation, something which would be expected from a supervisor.

QUESTION 7

1. As soon as there becomes a natural break in her talk, raise your hand and explain that you are finding it difficult to understand most of what she is saying. Respectfully ask if she would please slow down so that you can take in all of the important information she is relaying.

Answer: Effective

Explanation: This is efficient, as it is important that you understand what is being said at the meeting. If you wait until the end, your manager will have to go through the entire meeting again.

2. Wait until the end of the meeting and then ask your work colleagues for clarification on what she was saying.

Answer: Fairly Effective

Explanation: This is fairly effective, as you are seeking help from your other colleagues.

3. Wait to the end of the meeting before speaking to her in private and explain to her that you didn't understand most of what she was saying.

Answer: Ineffective

Explanation: This is ineffective. Yes, you will get to hear everything that was said at the meeting; however, your manager will have to repeat all of the meeting points again, which will take considerable time.

4. Do nothing

Answer: Counterproductive

Explanation: This is counterproductive, as you will never get to understand what was said during the meeting.

QUESTION 8

1. Challenge her in a respectable manner and say that you think she is wrong for saying these things about a senior member of the team.

Answer: Fairly Effective

Explanation: This is fairly effective, as you are standing your ground and being firm about how you feel other members of the organisation are treated.

2. Thank her for the information and be on your guard from now on when dealing with my manager.

Answer: Ineffective

Explanation: This is ineffective. Whilst it may appear to be a good thing that you have taken on-board her comments, it is not okay to pre-judge people based on the comments or viewpoints of just one person.

3. Thank her for the information but explain that you do not want to pre-judge people and you want to have an entirely open mind. You will take him as you find him.

Answer: Effective

Explanation: This is effective, as it shows that you are not prepared to pre-judge people. After all, she may have a personal grudge against the manager and be deliberately trying to cause him harm.

4. Thank her for the information and then ask other people within the organisation if they have had the same experience whilst working with your manager.

Answer: Counterproductive.

Explanation: You could end up discussing what you have heard with a member of the team who is close/supportive of the manager, and the gossip could get back to him, which might not be good for your future prospects.

QUESTION 9

1. Speak to your colleague in private and ask him whether anything is wrong. You would also offer your support to see if you can help him through this difficult period he is going through.

Answer: Effective

Explanation: This is effective, as you are asking your colleague if there is anything wrong. Your colleague is likely to feel supported. This would be the best way to handle this type of situation.

2. Approach your manager in confidence and tell him that you think there might be something wrong with your work colleague that is having an impact on his work performance.

Answer: Fairly Effective

Explanation: This is fairly effective, as you are raising your concerns with your manager and making him aware that there may be something more going on than first meets the eye. It is not effective, as it's not really your place to get involved.

3. Do nothing. You do not want to interfere as it is not your problem.

Answer: Counterproductive

Explanation: This is counterproductive. You are aware there is an issue, yet you are choosing to do nothing about it.

4. Speak to your work colleague and offer to do some of his work for him in order to ease the pressure he is under from his manager.

Answer: Ineffective

Explanation: This an ineffective response, as it does nothing to resolve the poor performance your colleague has been reprimanded for.

QUESTION 10

Complete the 6-month supervision period as planned and don't say anything about how you feel.

Answer: Ineffective

Explanation: This is ineffective, as it is important to speak to your manager about your frustrations

2. Tell your work colleagues how you feel and get their advice on what they think you should do.

Answer: Fairly Effective

Explanation: This is a fairly effective response. However, remember that whilst there is nothing wrong with speaking to your work colleagues, they are not the ones in the position to make a change to your supervised working.

3. Start working more on your own without telling anyone.

Answer: Counterproductive

Explanation: This is counterproductive. Your line manager would be extremely disappointed if you started working unsupervised, against his instructions. This could also lead to discipline procedures against you.

4. Arrange a meeting with your line manager to explain how you now feel ready to work more on your own, unsupervised. Ask his permission for the supervision period to come to an end.

Answer: Effective

Explanation: This is effective, as you are discussing how you feel with your line manager. He can then make the decision on whether or not to reduce the time period that you are supervised.

QUESTION 11

1. Explain to your team member that the group need her, and that she should rise above it and continue with the project.

Answer: Ineffective

Explanation: This is ineffective. Even though it will boost your team member's confidence, this does not deal with the current situation.

2. Wait to see if you hear anything as mentioned by the individual, and then take action.

Answer: Counterproductive

Explanation: This is counterproductive. Waiting to see if anything happens is not dealing with the current situation. It shows that you do not believe your team member, and shows a lack of initiative at handling difficult situations.

3. Sit the individual in question down, and ask their side of the story.

Answer: Fairly Effective

Explanation: This option is fairly effective. Sitting the individual in question down, and asking their side of the story shows that you are working towards resolving the issue by gaining a full understanding of what is happening.

4. Sit them both down to try and resolve the issue, before continuing on with the project.

Answer: Effective

Explanation: This is effective. Sitting both team members down, and discussing how to resolve the situation, not only shows professionalism, but it also handles the situation in a mature and efficient manner.

QUESTION 12

1. *Tell the oncoming shift workers that they will have to work on their own, unsupervised, for 30 minutes until their supervisor arrives.*

Answer: Ineffective

Explanation: This is ineffective. Teamwork is important, and you should be prepared to wait for the oncoming shift supervisor.

2. Call your girlfriend and tell her you will be late coming home. Then, supervise the oncoming shift workers until their supervisor arrives.

Answer: Effective

Explanation: This is effective, and constitutes what would be expected of a supervisor in this type of role.

3. Call your boss and ask her what she thinks you should do.

Answer: Fairly Effective

Explanation: This is fairly effective. That being said, your boss is likely to ask if you will wait for the oncoming supervisor to arrive anyway, so you may as well stay on and wait for him.

4. Just leave at the end of your shift. The fact that he is going to be late is not your problem.

Answer: Counterproductive

Explanation: This is a counterproductive response, as you are not even informing the oncoming shift workers that their supervisor will be late.

QUESTION 13

1. Explain that you cannot meet their request as you have lots of paperwork work to catch up on.

Answer: Counterproductive

Explanation: This is counterproductive, as it does nothing to help out the head office.

2. Explain to head office that you have lots of paperwork to catch up on and ask them how they want you to prioritise your work.

Answer: Ineffective

Explanation: This is ineffective. You are a manager and you should be able to work out how to prioritise your own workload. This shows a lack of professionalism and initiative.

3. Tell head office that you have lots of paperwork to catch up on but that you are prepared to ring around the other depots in the region to see if there is another manager available to go to the depot. If not, then you would be prepared to go and you would have to catch up with your paperwork another time.

Answer: Fairly Effective

Explanation: This is fairly effective, as you are offering to ring around to find another manager to cover. Failing that, you are still happy to take up the task.

4. Agree to go to the depot for the rest of the day and take your paperwork with you to do, whilst you are there.

Answer: Effective

Explanation: This is effective, as you are agreeing to go to the depot and you will work on your paperwork whilst you are there.

QUESTION 14

1. Apologise for the inconvenience that has been caused through the defective shaver. Explain to the customer the company's refund policy and that a receipt is required for a refund or exchange. However, explain to him that, if he can provide proof of purchase, by way of a card statement, that you will ask your manager if you can exchange the shaver for him.

Answer: Effective

Explanation: This is efficient. Although a receipt is required for exchange or refund, you are using your initiative and trying to find an alternative solution to rectify the problem.

2. Explain to him that, because he does not have a receipt, you are not able to help him.

Answer: Counterproductive

Explanation: This is counterproductive. Although you are correct in the fact that he needs a receipt in order to exchange the defective shaver, you are doing nothing at all to solve the problem.

3. Apologise for the inconvenience that has been caused through the defective shaver and then happily exchange the defective shaver for a new one.

Answer: Ineffective

Explanation: This is ineffective. You cannot exchange the shaver until you have proof that it has been purchased from your store.

4. Ask your manager what he thinks you should do.

Answer: Fairly Effective

Explanation: This is fairly effective. Due to your position as a retail assistant, it is good practice to ask your manager for advice.

QUESTION 15

1. Explain to your boss that the presentation is being presented that afternoon, and ask him for ideas on how to implement this information in time.

Answer: Fairly Effective

Explanation: This is a fairly effective response. You are clearly explaining the situation to your boss, and asking him for advice.

2. Inform your boss that whilst you cannot add in this information due to time constraints, you will be happy to answer any questions they have.

Answer: Ineffective

Explanation: While inviting people in to ask questions at the end of the interview, this will not demonstrate all of the important information that has been missed in the presentation. This doesn't fix your presentation, and will suggest that you ran out of time to complete it

3. Ignore your boss's concerns and present the presentation the way it is.

Answer: Counterproductive

Explanation: Ignoring your boss's comments regarding the presentation does not fix the issues, nor does it deal with the situation.

4. Ask your colleagues to help you with the additional information, so that you can ensure the work gets added.

Answer: Effective

Explanation: This is an effective response. Asking for help from your colleagues will allow you to get the extra information added in time for the presentation. It shows that you are willing to take help from other people, and will therefore be able to complete the presentation to a better standard.

Civil Service
Situational Judgement
Test 3

Read the following scenarios and then rate the effectiveness of each response. For example, if you believe that response 1 is counterproductive, you should place a 1 in the counterproductive box.

You have 20 minutes to complete the 15 questions.

QUESTION 1

You are a parking attendant patrolling a car park. At 10 past 10 in the morning, you are performing your hourly ticket inspection. You come across a man returning to his vehicle who has not purchased a ticket. He claims that the reason for this is because he had to quickly get some money from the bank. It's an emergency as his mother has taken a fall and is in hospital. He has the money to pay for the ticket there and then. What do you do?

1. Consult with the other people in the car park as to what to do.
2. Allow him to pay for the ticket.
3. Perform a citizen's arrest. This man is a criminal.
4. Issue the man with a standard penalty fare.

Effective	
Fairly Effective	
Ineffective	
Counterproductive	

QUESTION 2

> Your company has recently hired a new staff member. He has only been working for you for 2 days, but you have noticed him making inappropriate remarks towards female staff members. Your manager does not seem to have noticed. One of your female colleagues has confessed that his behaviour makes her feel uncomfortable, but she does not want to risk jeopardising the employee's future, especially since he has only just joined the company. Another female staff member claims that the next time he does it, she will 'give him a smack'. What do you do?
>
> 1. Take the new employee to one side and tell him that his behaviour needs to change.
>
> 2. Go to your manager and explain the situation.
>
> 3. Encourage your female colleagues to speak to your manager.
>
> 4. Ignore the behaviour. He's only joking.

Effective	
Fairly Effective	
Ineffective	
Counterproductive	

QUESTION 3

You are the customer service assistant in a shopping centre. Two men approach you, arguing furiously. One of the men approaches you, claiming that the other man took his bag. The other man says that the bag was his all along, and that the first man is lying. He states 'finder's keepers'. You ask the man to hand over the bag to you, so that the CCTV footage of the centre can be reviewed. This leaves the first man irate. As you turn around to deal with him, the second man runs off with the bag, jumps into a taxi, and is gone. What do you do?

1. Offer to take the man's contact details, so that he can be reimbursed for the price of some of his shopping.

2. Tell the man there is nothing that you can do, tell him to contact the police.

3. Report the incident to senior management. Tell the man that your company will be in touch.

4. Take the man into a private room where you can write up a report of the incident, which will then be passed on to the police.

Effective	
Fairly Effective	
Ineffective	
Counterproductive	

QUESTION 4

You are the centre manager for a well-known writing retreat in the English countryside. Part of your role is ensuring that the centre is well staffed, food goes out on time and that the centre is kept clean and tidy. You have recently taken on a new staff member, who is struggling with his position. Today you have discovered that the new staff member has forgotten to pre-order food supplies, meaning that there is no way to cook dinner for the course attendees that evening. The staff member is fairly upset at his mistake. What do you say to him?

1. 'Pack your bags. You're sacked'

2. 'Mistakes happen. Let's pull the team together and brainstorm some ideas as to how we can fix this.'

3. 'Maybe you should consider whether this is the right position for you.'

4. 'Okay, obviously this isn't ideal, but let's think of some solutions. We'll have a serious chat about this at the end of the day though.'

Effective	
Fairly Effective	
Ineffective	
Counterproductive	

QUESTION 5

You are working as a bus driver and it is coming to the end of your shift. In 5 minutes' time, you are due to sign off and head home. Your line manager approaches you and asks you to mop the bus depot floor before you go off duty. You realise that this will take you 15 minutes to do the job professionally. What would you do?

1. Carry out the task as requested, professionally, even though it will mean that you have to stay behind at work for an additional 10 minutes.

2. Inform your manager that you are happy to complete the task, but ask if you can finish slightly earlier tomorrow to compensate.

3. Carry out the task to a slightly lesser standard, therefore finishing your shift on time.

4. Politely refuse to carry out the task.

Effective	
Fairly Effective	
Ineffective	
Counterproductive	

QUESTION 6

You are working as an admin assistant in a council office. It is a very busy day in the office and everyone is working flat out dealing with an annual task. You are walking towards the back of the office through the storage area to take your 10 minute tea break, when you notice that the contents of a large shelf have all fallen on the floor. You estimate it would take you at least 10 minutes to put all of the contents back on the shelf. What would you do?

1. Walk around the contents and go for your tea break. You are legally entitled to a break and someone else will be able to clear up the mess.

2. Inform your manager that you are going to put the contents back on the shelf and request that you take your 10 minute tea break after the job is complete.

3. Inform your manager that the contents have fallen on the floor, and ask him if he can find someone else to put the contents back on the shelf, as you are about to go on your tea break.

4. Forget about your tea break and put the contents back on the shelf yourself.

Effective	
Fairly Effective	
Ineffective	
Counterproductive	

QUESTION 7

> You are the supervisor of a small team working for a local council service. It is December and it's the busiest time of the year. Your team is snowed under with work and some of the team members are clearly feeling the strain. You have a team development meeting booked for the forthcoming Tuesday morning. However, one of the team members approaches you and tells you that she won't be at the meeting as she is too busy to attend. What would you do?
>
> 1. Spend time with the team member to identify ways in which she can manage her time more efficiently so that she can attend the team development meeting.
>
> 2. Tell the team member that the team development meeting is mandatory. She must attend.
>
> 3. Tell the team member that you understand how she is feeling and that she does not need to attend the team development meeting.
>
> 4. Get a member of staff from another team to cover the team member's workload during the day of the meeting so that she can attend.

Effective	
Fairly Effective	
Ineffective	
Counterproductive	

QUESTION 8

You have noticed one of your colleagues continuously turning up to work with a hangover. You haven't said anything before, but you've realised that the situation is becoming more frequent. Today at work, the same colleague has turned up to work, and you can smell alcohol on their breath. The colleague is disruptive, loud, and is clearly still intoxicated. What would you do?

1. You tell your colleague that he is being extremely unprofessional and tell him to arrange a lift home and sober up.

2. You inform your colleague that you are aware of the said issue, and encourage him to seek help.

3. You get another one of your colleagues to drive him home, so you can continue working in peace.

4. You tell him to make a cup of coffee and sober up, and get on with his work quietly.

Effective	
Fairly Effective	
Ineffective	
Counterproductive	

QUESTION 9

Recently, your company's fortunes seem to have taken a turn for the worse. Profits are at an all-time low, employees seem to be underperforming and your sales manager refuses to accept any of the blame. He claims that the bad results are out of his control, and that the products being produced are simply of poor quality. Privately, he has also informed you that he believes customers are being scared off by current employee sales techniques, and as a result won't purchase from the organisation. During a recent team meeting, one of your colleagues tried to raise her concerns. Your sales manager lambasted her, branding her weak and naive. Your colleague was extremely upset by this behaviour, and is considering making a complaint of sexism to the chairman of the company. Although in your opinion there is no evidence to suggest this, she has asked you to act as a witness to her statement. What do you do?

1. Agree to act as a witness, but tell the chairman that there is no evidence to suggest sexism.

2. Tell the chairman that you believe your sales manager was acting in a sexist manner.

3. Agree to act a witness. Suggest to the chairman that the department needs some extra help.

4. Encourage your colleague to sue the company. Sexism is unacceptable.

Effective	
Fairly Effective	
Ineffective	
Counterproductive	

QUESTION 10

You are working for a leisure centre as a customer assistant. Part of your job is to assist disabled customers in and out of the building. It is the middle of a weekday, and therefore there are very few customers to deal with. On the other side of the building, you notice a well-known celebrity. One of your colleagues has noticed this too, and suggests that you both go over to the other side to get her autograph. What do you do?

1. Agree to cross over and get an autograph. This could be your only chance to meet such a prestigious person.

2. Tell your colleague that you won't be going anywhere. What they do is up to them.

3. Refuse to go, and encourage your colleague to do the same. This would be unprofessional.

4. Take mobile pictures of the celebrity from afar, but don't approach them.

Effective	
Fairly Effective	
Ineffective	
Counterproductive	

QUESTION 11

You're working as a shop assistant in a toy shop. A woman approaches you and asks for help locating a particular brand of toy. She informs you that the toy is showing 'IN STOCK' on the company website and that she has travelled 10 miles to buy it. After searching for 10 minutes you establish that the toy is out of stock and the information on the website is incorrect. What would you do?

1. Apologise to the customer and say you are sorry but there is nothing more you can do.

2. Apologise to the customer and inform her that there is another branch 15 miles away in the next town. If she travels there, they have the toy she wants in stock.

3. Apologise unreservedly for the toy not being in stock. Tell her that you will order the toy immediately from your supplier and then deliver it to her home as soon as it arrives. She will not be charged for either the toy or the delivery due to the inconvenience and stress caused.

4. Apologise unreservedly for the toy not being in stock. Tell her that you will order the toy immediately from your supplier and then deliver it to her home as soon as it arrives. She will be charged for the toy, but not for the delivery, due to the inconvenience and stress caused.

Effective	
Fairly Effective	
Ineffective	
Counterproductive	

QUESTION 12

You are working as a refuse lorry driver collecting waste from customers' homes. Whilst attending someone's home collect their rubbish, they offer you £10 as a thank you for being prompt and for giving an excellent service. The council has a strict policy which states that you must not take any form of tip or financial reward from customers whilst at work. What would you do?

1. Thank them for the money, put it in your pocket, and leave a happy person. Nobody will ever know that you took the money, so there's no harm.

2. Thank them for the money, but explain that you are unable to accept tips or financial rewards of this nature. Tell them that if they would like to give a reward, the council supports local charities and they will be able to donate via their website.

3. Thank them for their kind offer, but explain that you are unable to accept tips or financial rewards of this nature.

4. Walk away and ignore them.

Effective	
Fairly Effective	
Ineffective	
Counterproductive	

QUESTION 13

You are working alone as a volunteer at a local homeless shelter. It is a Saturday evening and there is a large queue of people waiting to be served. All of a sudden the coffee machine breaks down and you will be unable to serve coffee for the rest of the day. You will still be able to serve soft drinks and tea. What would you do?

1. Apologise to the people in the queue and inform them you will not be able to serve them due to the breakdown of the coffee machine, which is beyond your control. Then, close the shelter and make your way home.

2. Apologise to the people in the queue and inform them that you will only be able to serve soft drinks and tea due to the breakdown of the coffee machine. Then, create a sign that says 'COFFEE MACHINE BROKEN – WE ARE ONLY ABLE TO SERVE SOFT DRINKS AND TEA – APOLOGIES FOR ANY INCONVENIENCE CAUSED' and place it on the shelter door so that people can make a decision whether or not they want to come in.

3. Apologise to each person as they reach the front of the queue and explain to them that you are unable to serve coffee but that you can serve them soft drinks or tea.

4. Call your boss and ask her what she wants you to do.

Effective	
Fairly Effective	
Ineffective	
Counterproductive	

QUESTION 14

You are on the way to your shift at your office, but get stuck in traffic. A sign above the motorway indicates that you are going to be delayed well beyond your starting time.

1. Call the office and let them know about the situation. Promise to be in as soon as possible.

2. Call your colleague and ask him to cover the start of your shift.

3. Just get into work when you can. It's not your fault if there's traffic.

4. Call your manager on his mobile. It's best to let him know as soon as possible.

Effective	
Fairly Effective	
Ineffective	
Counterproductive	

QUESTION 15

You arrive into work at 5 to 9. Your shift will start at 9am. When you arrive in, the receptionist approaches you:

Receptionist: *'Hey, can you pop down to the shops and pick up some milk, please? We've run out and nobody can have tea.'*

1. 'Sorry, my shift begins in 5 minutes, and I need to prepare for it. You'll have to find someone else.'

2. 'I don't drink tea, so you'll have to find someone else to do it.'

3. 'That's fine, but I'll be late for my shift. Hopefully that's okay.'

4. 'Let me ask the manager if it's okay for me to go. If so, sure, I'd be happy to.'

Effective	
Fairly Effective	
Ineffective	
Counterproductive	

SUGGESTED ANSWERS AND EXPLANATIONS
QUESTION 1

1. Consult with the other people in the car park as to what to do.

Answer: Ineffective

Explanation: This is unprofessional. It's nothing to do with the other people in the car park, and they shouldn't have to tell you how to do your job.

2. Allow him to pay the full ticket fare to his intended stop.

Answer: Fairly Effective

Explanation: This is fairly effective, in the sense that you are showing compassion and common sense. However, technically the man is breaking the law by not buying a ticket first.

3. Perform a citizen's arrest. This man is a criminal.

Answer: Counterproductive

Explanation: This is counterproductive. The man has done nothing to warrant a citizen's arrest, and certainly does not appear to be dangerous or in need of restraint.

4. Issue the man with a standard penalty fare.

Answer: Effective

Explanation: Regardless of his personal circumstances, the man has broken the rules, and therefore you need to issue him with a penalty fare.

QUESTION 2

1. Take the new employee to one side and tell him that his behaviour needs to change.

Answer: Effective

Explanation: This is an effective response. You are taking steps to try and amend the situation, without going to management straight away. By discussing it with the new employee to one side, you are not humiliating them in front of your other colleagues.

2. Go to your manager and explain the situation.

Answer: Ineffective

Explanation: This is an inefficient response, as the woman has already said that she does not want to jeopardise the employee's position at the company. Therefore it is not up to you to go to management.

3. Encourage your female colleagues to speak to your manager.

Answer: Fairly Effective

Explanation: This is fairly effective, as it is the right thing to do. Although you should of course take some responsibility for helping your colleagues, ultimately it is their issue to take to the manager

4. Ignore the behaviour. He's only joking.

Answer: Counterproductive

Explanation: This is counterproductive. Sexual harassment/inappropriateness is a serious issue.

QUESTION 3

1. Offer to take the man's contact details, so that he can be reimbursed for the price of some of his shopping.

Answer: Ineffective

Explanation: This is ineffective. The man does not need to be reimbursed for his shopping, he just wants his bag back.

2. Tell the man there is nothing that you can do, tell him to contact the police.

Answer: Counterproductive

Explanation: This is counterproductive. You are being extremely unsympathetic and unprofessional, along with refusing to take any responsibility.

3. Report the incident to senior management. Tell the man that your company will be in touch.

Answer: Fairly Effective

Explanation: This is fairly effective, as it demonstrates that you are taking reasonable action in order to resolve the issue. Whilst you have been quite vague in terms of getting in contact with him, it still shows that you are acting upon it by going to management.

4. Take the man into a private room where you can write up a report of the incident, which will then be passed on to the police.

Answer: Effective

Explanation: This is effective, as it means that you have taken initiative, acted in a responsible manner and then passed the matter over to the organisation best equipped to deal with it. Along with this, you have made the man feel reassured that the case is in good hands.

QUESTION 4

1. 'Pack your bags. You're sacked.'

Answer: Counterproductive

Explanation: Sacking the employee on the spot won't solve anything, and would be unprofessional.

2. 'Mistakes happen. Let's pull the team together and brainstorm some ideas as to how we can fix this.'

Answer: Fairly Effective

Explanation: This is a fairly effective as it allows you to try and reach a positive solution to the situation, whilst gaining suggestions from a wide variety of people.

3. 'Maybe you should consider whether this is the right position for you.'

Answer: Ineffective

Explanation: This is an ineffective response. There will be time to discuss this after the incident has been resolved. All this will do is damage the employee's confidence, making him less likely to successfully complete future tasks.

4. 'Okay, obviously this isn't ideal, but let's think of some solutions. We'll have a serious chat about this at the end of the day though.'

Answer: Effective

Explanation: This is an efficient response. You are treating the issue in a constructive manner, but still ensuring that the employee knows that it's a serious mistake.

QUESTION 5

1. Carry out the task as requested, professionally, even though it will mean that you have to stay behind at work for an additional 10 minutes.

Answer: Effective

Explanation: This is effective, as you are willing to stay behind and do the job to the standard required, something which will be appreciated by your line manager.

2. Inform your manager that you are happy to complete the task, but ask if you can finish slightly earlier tomorrow to compensate.

Answer: Fairly Effective

Explanation: This is a fairly effective response, as you are completing the task, but still explaining the situation to your manager.

3. Carry out the task to a slightly lesser standard, therefore finishing your shift on time.

Answer: Ineffective

Explanation: This is an ineffective response. Although you are agreeing to do the task, you are not carrying it out to the required standard.

4. Politely refuse to carry out the task.

Answer: Counterproductive

Explanation: This is counterproductive, as the task will not get done, and the workplace will be left untidy for the oncoming shift.

QUESTION 6

1. Walk around the contents and go for my tea break. You are legally entitled to a break and someone else will be able to clear up the mess.

Answer: Counterproductive

Explanation: This is counterproductive. Whilst you are entitled to your tea break, you are doing nothing about the issue. At the very least you should inform your manager so that someone else can start tidying up the mess.

2. Inform your manager that you are going to put the contents back on the shelf and request that you take your 10-minute tea break after the job is complete.

Answer: Effective

Explanation: This is an effective response. Not only are you taking immediate action by putting the contents back on the shelf, but you are also ensuring that you get your tea break.

3. Inform your manager that the contents have fallen on the floor, and ask him if he can find someone else to put the contents back on the shelf, as you are about to go on your tea break.

Answer: Ineffective

Explanation: This is inefficient. Although you are informing your manager about the problem, everybody is really busy with the task, and they will not be able to put the contents back on the shelf.

4. Forget about your tea break and put the contents back on the shelf yourself.

Answer: Fairly Effective

Explanation: This is a fairly effective response, as you are dealing with the problem. That being said, you still need to find the time to take your break. If you don't do this, then you will tire faster during the rest of the day, and you may not perform to the best of your ability.

QUESTION 7

1. Spend time with the team member to identify ways in which she can manage her time efficiently so that she can attend the team development meeting.

Answer: Effective

Explanation: This is effective, as you are showing support to the team member, and you are also identifying ways to manage her time.

2. Tell the team member that the team development meeting is mandatory. She must attend.

Answer: Ineffective

Explanation: This is ineffective, as it will only add stress to how she is feeling. It is not the most professional way to handle the situation.

3. Tell the team member that you understand how she is feeling and that she does not need to attend the team development meeting.

Answer: Counterproductive

Explanation: This is counterproductive, as you are failing to tackle the reasons why she is unable to cope with the increased workload. She is then more likely not to attend future meetings if she feels you give her permission not to attend. This also demonstrates to the other team members that it is OK to skip team meetings.

4. Get a member of staff from another team to cover the team member's workload during the day of the meeting so that she can attend.

Answer: Fairly Effective

Explanation: This is fairly effective, as it allows the team member to attend the team development meeting whilst her work is getting done.

QUESTION 8

1. You tell your colleague that he is being extremely unprofessional and tell him to arrange a lift home and sober up.

Answer: Effective

Explanation: This is effective. It is important that everyone remains safe, and an employee who is drunk could cause hazards. The employee needs to sober up before he can resume working.

2. You inform your colleague that you are aware of the said issue, and encourage him to seek help.

Answer: Fairly Effective

Explanation: This is fairly effective, as you are encouraging the man to get the right support.

3. You get another one of your colleagues to drive him home, so you can continue working in peace.

Answer: Ineffective

Explanation: This is inefficient. Getting another colleague to drive him home will cause further disruption to the workplace, and therefore is causing more disorder.

4. You tell him to make a cup of coffee and sober up, and get on with his work quietly.

Answer: Counterproductive

Explanation: This is counterproductive. An employee who is drunk is not going to perform their duties to the best of their ability, and this will compromise their work.

QUESTION 9

1. Agree to act as a witness, but tell the chairman that there is no evidence to suggest sexism.

Answer: Effective

Explanation: This is effective, as it is an honest response. If you have not seen any evidence of sexism, then you cannot support these claims. All you need to do is tell the chairman what you saw.

2. Tell the chairman that you believe your sales manager was acting in a sexist manner.

Answer: Ineffective

Explanation: This is ineffective. As the passage states, you have seen no evidence of sexism.

3. Agree to act a witness. Suggest to the chairman that the department needs some extra help.

Answer: Fairly Effective

Explanation: This is a fairly effective response, as you are agreeing to act as a witness, and offering some advice on how to fix other difficult issues. That being said, you haven't been brought into the meeting to discuss the latter.

4. Encourage your colleague to sue the company. Sexism is unacceptable.

Answer: Counterproductive

Explanation: This is counterproductive. Not only have you seen no evidence of sexism, but suing the company would be a fairly extreme course of action.

QUESTION 10

1. Agree to cross over and get an autograph. This could be your only chance to meet such a prestigious person.

Answer: Counterproductive

Explanation: This is counterproductive. It would be extremely unprofessional to abandon your post just to go and get an autograph. Furthermore, the celebrity might not want to be harassed.

2. Tell your colleague that you won't be going anywhere. What they do is up to them.

Answer: Fairly Effective

Explanation: This demonstrates that you are following the rules and standards expected of you. You are not the keeper of your other colleague, so you cannot force them to stay.

3. Refuse to go, and encourage your colleague to do the same. This would be unprofessional.

Answer: Effective

Explanation: This is effective. It would be extremely unprofessional to abandon your post just to go and get an autograph. Furthermore, the person might not want to be harassed. The fact that you have encouraged your colleague to do the same shows that you are thinking in the best interests of the company.

4. Take mobile pictures of the celebrity from afar, but don't approach them.

Answer: Ineffective

Explanation: This is an ineffective response. Although you aren't leaving your post, you are acting unprofessionally.

QUESTION 11

1. Apologise to the customer and say you are sorry but there is nothing more you can do.

Answer: Counterproductive

Explanation: This is counterproductive. Although you are apologising, you are doing nothing to resolve the issue, or rectify the mistake made by the shop.

2. Apologise to the customer and inform her that there is another toy shop 15 miles away in the next town. If she travels there, they might have the toy she wants in stock.

Answer: Fairly effective

Explanation: This is fairly effective. Although it is unfortunate that the woman will need to travel so far, you are clearly explaining where she can go to obtain the toy.

3. Apologise unreservedly for the toy not being in stock. Tell her that you will order the toy immediately from your supplier and then deliver it to her home as soon as it arrives. She will not be charged for either the toy or the delivery due to the inconvenience and stress caused.

Answer: Ineffective

Explanation: This is ineffective. Although you are being helpful and polite, the woman still needs to pay for the toy. Giving it to her for free is not the right response, since your company have not done anything wrong.

4. Apologise unreservedly for the toy not being in stock. Tell her that you will order the toy immediately from your supplier and then deliver it to her home as soon as it arrives. She will be charged for the toy, but not for the delivery, due to the inconvenience and stress caused.

Answer: Effective

Explanation: This is efficient, as you are ordering the toy for her and delivering it direct to her. Although she has to pay for the toy you have agreed to deliver it for free, to compensate for the wasted journey. This will hopefully avoid any ill-feeling on the customer's part and will go part-way to making good the mistake made by the shop.

QUESTION 12

1. Thank them for the money, put it in your pocket, and leave a happy person. Nobody will ever know that you took the money, so there's no harm.

Answer: Counterproductive

Explanation: This is counterproductive. You are in breach of the company's strict policies regarding tips and financial rewards, and you could be dismissed or disciplined for breaking this.

2. Thank them for the money, but explain that you are unable to accept tips or financial rewards of this nature. Tell them that if they would like to give a reward, the council supports local charities and they will be able to donate via their website.

Answer: Effective

Explanation: This is effective, as you are politely refusing the generous offer, whilst not placing yourself in danger of being in breach of the company's strict policies regarding tips and financial rewards. Yet you are still giving the customer the option to donate to the supermarkets chosen charity.

3. Thank them for their kind offer, but explain that you are unable to accept tips or financial rewards of this nature.

Answer: Fairly Effective

Explanation: This is fairly effective, as you are politely refusing the generous offer whilst not placing yourself in danger of being in breach of the company's strict policies, regarding tips and financial rewards.

4. Walk away and ignore them.

Answer: Ineffective

Explanation: This is inefficient. Whilst you are not placing yourself in danger of being in breach of the company's strict policies regarding tips and financial rewards, the way in which you are handling the situation is rude, and will leave the customer feeling devalued and upset.

QUESTION 13

1. Apologise to the people in the queue and inform them you will not be able to serve them due to the breakdown of the coffee machine, which is beyond your control. Then, close the shelter and make your way home.

Answer: Counterproductive

Explanation: This is a counterproductive response. Whilst you are apologising to the customers, you are not offering them an alternative drink. You are simply giving up and going home.

2. Apologise to the people in the queue and inform them that you will only be able to serve soft drinks and tea due to the breakdown of the coffee machine. Then, create a sign that says 'COFFEE MACHINE BROKEN – WE ARE ONLY ABLE TO SERVE SOFT DRINKS AND TEA – APOLOGIES FOR ANY INCONVENIENCE CAUSED' and place it on the shelter door front so that people can make a decision whether or not they want to come in.

Answer: Effective

Explanation: This is effective. Not only are you apologising to the customers, you are also offering people an alternative drink and you are also informing people of the issue before they enter the shop. This will save you considerable time having to explain to everyone who comes into the shelter of the issue.

3. Apologise to each person as they reach the front of the queue and explain to them that you are unable to serve coffee but that you can serve them soft drinks or tea.

Answer: Fairly Effective

Explanation: Although you will need to repeat yourself each time someone comes into the shelter, you are still staying open and offering alternative drinks.

4. Call your boss and ask her what she wants you to do.

Answer: Ineffective

Explanation: This an ineffective response. Yes, you are doing something about the problem, but you are not working on your own initiative. You don't need to call your boss about this.

QUESTION 14

1. Call the office and let them know about the situation. Promise to be in as soon as possible.

Answer: Effective

Explanation: This is a very effective response. You are giving the plenty of notice about the situation, ensuring they can make preparations for your delay.

2. Call your colleague and ask him to cover the start of your shift.

Answer: Ineffective

Explanation: This is an ineffective response. You should simply call the office and let them know that you will be late, rather than asking your colleague to disrupt his own working schedule.

3. Just get into work when you can. It's not your fault if there's traffic.

Answer: Counterproductive

Explanation: This is a counterproductive response. You need to let the office know that you will be late.

4. Call your manager on his mobile. It's best to let him know as soon as possible.

Answer: Fairly Effective

Explanation: This is a fairly effective, if slightly unnecessary, response. It's good that you've taken the initiative to let your manager know, but really you only need to contact the office.

QUESTION 15

1. 'Sorry, my shift begins in 5 minutes, and I need to prepare for it. You'll have to find someone else.'

Answer: Fairly Effective

Explanation: This is a fairly effective, although somewhat rude, response.

2. 'I don't drink tea, so you'll have to find someone else to do it.'

Answer: Ineffective

Explanation: This is rude, and doesn't give a proper explanation for why you can't complete the task.

3. 'That's fine, but I'll be late for my shift. Hopefully that's okay.'

Answer: Counterproductive

Explanation: This is an counterproductive response. You need to gain the permission of the manager as you can't be late for your shift without his/her consent.

4. 'Let me ask my manager if it's okay for me to go. If so, sure, I'd be happy to.'

Answer: Effective

Explanation: This is an effective response. Before you commit to this task, you should certainly check with your manager first. Being late for your shift could cause serious problems.

Numerical Reasoning Test

During the application process, you will be required to sit a number of psychometric tests which will include a numerical reasoning test. The idea of psychometric tests is to assess candidates on a number of different, assessable, relevant criteria. Psychometric tests do vary in their format and can range from simple numerical reasoning tests to more complicated job-specific tests.

What is a Numerical Reasoning Test?

Numerical reasoning tests come in vast range of different formats, and will assess your ability to work with numbers. Some of the standard types of tests will include basic arithmetic questions, addition, subtraction, multiplication and division. Other tests may include more complicated sums such as algebra, percentages equations, areas and many more. Much of the time you will be assessed against a mixture of all mathematical disciplines. This will also be dependent on the role and the organisation you are applying for.

Choosing Your Answers

The answer format of the tests can vary. You may be asked to complete a sum and input your answer directly onto paper or via a computer. Your test may be a multiple choice assessment, which is one of the more common formats used by many organisations, when assessing candidates.

Samples Formats of Numerical Questions

Try the following sample questions of how a numerical reasoning tests maybe laid out and presented to you during a test. You can check your answers on the following pages.

Question 1

329 + 234 = ?

Answer

Question 2

500 ÷ 2 = ?

Answer

Question 3

28 × 2 = ?

Answer

Question 4

A square field has a perimeter of 72cm. What is the area of the square field?

Answer

Question 5

How many grams are there in 2.5 kilograms?

A	B	C	D
0.0025g	250g	2005g	2500g

Question 6

Josh, Gemma and Alex all went for lunch. The final bill came to £78.60. They decide to split the bill evenly. How much does each person pay?

A	B	C	D
£23.40	£38.10	£26.20	£19.80

Question 7

Below shows a list of quotes for importing wood. The quotes cover different periods of time. Theses quotes are for the cost of importing woods.

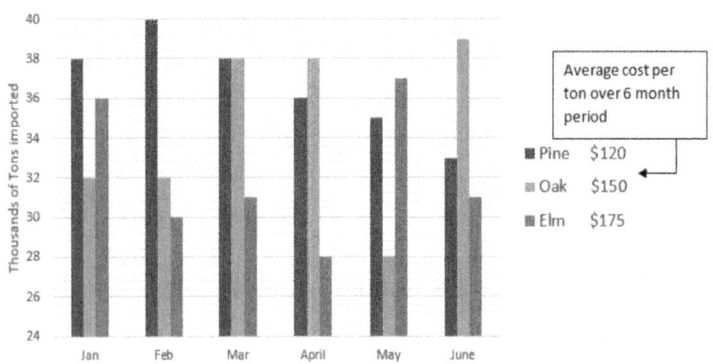

7a. What was the difference in thousands of tons between oak and elm imports in the first 3 months of the year?

A	B	C	D
2	5	4	6

7b. What was the total value of oak wood ($) imported over the 6 month period?

A	B	C	D
31,050	42,550	32,500	30,050

Question 8

The Lionhare Plastics Company have put out a notice for staff to enrol onto training courses. Below are quotes from 3 suppliers.

Academic training course	College 1 Total cost over 4 years (£)	College 2 Total cost over 2 years (£)	College 3 Total cost over 6 years (£)
PR and Advertising	14,500	8,350	34,500
Finances	18,250	8,750	42,750
Social Media	24,050	13,000	72,000

8a. What percentage of the total quote provided by College 2 accounts for Social Media training?

A	B	C	D
40.1%	45.6%	43.2%	44.5%

8b. Based on an annual one year cost, which college provides the cheapest overall quote for the PR and Advertising course?

A	B	C	D
College 1	College 2	College 3	All the same

As you can see from the above examples, there are a number of ways that the questions can be presented to you. These are only a few of. There are literally masses of different question types but the above are some of the most common types.

Sample Questions – Answers and Explanations

Question 1. 329 + 234 = 563

Question 2. 500 ÷ 2 = 250

Question 3. 28 × 2 = 56

Question 4. 324 cm^2

As the shape is a square the sides will be the same length. 72 ÷ 4 = 18. Each length of the square is 18 cm. To work out the area = 18 x 18 = 324 cm^2.

Question 5. D (2,500g)

2.5 kg is equal 2,500 grams therefore the answer is D.

Question 6. C (£26.20)

To work out how much person pays we need to divide the total bill by three. £78.60 ÷ 3 = £26.20

Question 7a. B (5)

EOak; 32 + 32 + 38 = 102

Elm; 36 + 30 + 31 = 97

102 – 97 = 5

Question 7b. A (31,050)

32 + 32 + 38 + 38 + 38 + 39 = 207

207 × 150 = 31,050.

Question 8a. C (43.2%)

13,000 + 8,750 + 8,350 = 30,100

13,000 ÷ 30,100 × 100 = 43.18.

Rounded to 43.2%

Question 8b, A (College 1)

College 1; 14,500 ÷ 4 = 3,625.

College 2; 8,350 ÷ 2 = 4,175.

College 3; 34,500 ÷ 6 = 5,750.

The Civil Service Numerical Test Process

The numerical test you will have to sit as part of your application process, is an online test which you can undertake from the comfort of your own home. The purpose of this and any other Civil Service test is to assess you against a set of competencies called the Civil Service Success Profiles. For the numerical test the main one you are assessed against is the **Ability** profile. However, during the application process you will be assessed against each of the profiles on more than one occasion.

The Civil Service Numerical Test Structure

The Civil Service form of numerical test, will mainly comprise of data interpretation questions very similar to the last 2 practice questions, 7 & 8 from the sample questions in the previous section. The purpose of the assessment is to test your ability to perform calculations and be able to evaluate and decipher data to solve numerical problems.

Your questions will be presented to you via a table of data, a graph or chart of some description. You will then be asked a number of questions based on the information contained within the chart/table. The question will require you to make a calculation, such as calculating an average cost, or combining figures from a bar chart or table etc.

Taking the Civil Service Numerical Test

If you have been successful in your application this far, you will be invited to take the numerical test CSNT. As previously stated, the test is taken online. As soon as your invitation has been received you should start planning to take the test as soon as possible, to avoid missing the deadline for completion. However, you must ensure that you are fully prepared and have planned correctly for taking the assessment. There is a simple equation that you should follow; *Practice + Planning = Prepared.*

The first phase of your preparation is practice. You should ensure you have practiced a sufficient number of questions, and have a competent understanding of the types of questions, and be confident on how to answer these correctly. We have provided for you a number of practice questions within this starter guide. The Civil Service also provide a number of practice questions online, which you can also use to practice with.

For the second stage of your preparation, let us focus for a minute on the word **planning**. When deciding to take the test it is vital that you will be in a comfortable environment where you will not be disturbed by others, so you must plan this in advance. When planning please consider the following.

- Find a well-lit and quiet area, where you can sit comfortably to undertake the test using a PC or laptop.

- Allocate a time to do the test, when you are unlikely to be disturbed by others in your household.

- Plan to take the test when you are most mentally active. Do not take the test when you are most fatigued at the end of the day or under the influence of alcohol.

- Ensure you stay hydrated and eat a healthy meal prior to taking your test, this will aid your concentration levels.

- Ensure your internet connection is stable, the last thing you want is to lose your internet connection half way through your test.

- Have a pen & paper handy and also a calculator on hand for any complex calculations.

When you are ready to take the test, please read your invitation as full instructions will be given on how to proceed within the testing portal. The test itself is not timed so try to allocate as much time as required, do not rush. If you think the test will take an hour, allocate 2 hours. The tests are also adaptive based on your ongoing performance, if you get a question correct the next will be harder. The same will also be said if the you get a question incorrect the next question will be easier.

Scoring of the Test and Your Results

Upon completion of your test you will advised of your results, but not if you have passed or not.

The tests are scored dependent on the number of questions faced and also the difficulty of the test questions faced. Your score will then be compared to other candidates who have taken the same test. When you do receive your results, you will receive these as a percentile. This is not a percentage of questions answered correctly. This is based on your performance compared to the other candidates. For example, if you scored a percentile of 62%, this means that you scored higher than 62% of the other candidates.

All of the roles within the Civil Service are advertised to a certain level. If you have been successful at passing the minimum standard for the level of the role applying for, a number of things may happen. If the role you are applying for requires further tests, you will be sent an invitation to complete the further tests. After the deadline for the test has passed, the assessors will look at all of the candidates scores and will decide upon this what the roles pass mark will be.

After evaluating all results, the assessors can raise the pass mark, but this is generally dependent on the number of candidates amassing the passing score. If the assessors do decide to raise the score, you will be informed of this and if you have passed or not at the raised standard.

If at this time your application is not successful, but your test score has reached the minimum standard your score will be banked for 6 months and if you apply for roles of the same grade within the time frame, you will not have to resit the test.

Civil Service
Numerical Reasoning
Test 1

We have included for you below, some examples of the types of questions you will face during your CSNT. Please take this practice test, whenever you feel ready. Try to prepare for this practice test, like you would the real assessment, so please refer back at our tips from the 'Taking the Civil Service Numerical Test' section' within this guide.

For the following 12 questions, please study the information in the tables/charts provided and then select the correct answer from the answer choices available. The test is not timed and you may use a calculator if required.

Sample Question 1

A jewellery stall sold the following number of necklaces, watches and bracelets on the days of the week shown.

	MON	TUE	WED	THUR	FRI	SAT	SUN
Necklaces	12	42	32	4	6	24	36
Watches	3	11	10	8	2	4	12
Bracelets	17	18	6	34	32	12	40

1a What percentage of all jewellery items were sold on weekdays? To the nearest whole number.

A	B	C	D
60%	58%	62%	65%

1b How many more necklaces were sold than watches?

A	B	C	D
106	64	82	112

1c What was the ratio of the number of bracelets sold to the number of watches?

A	B	C	D
60:50	50:159	159:50	50:60

Sample Question 2

Lionhare council have put out a tender for electrical services. Below are quotes from 3 suppliers.

Electrical Services	Supplier 1 Total cost over 4 years (£)	Supplier 2 Total cost over 2 years (£)	Supplier 3 Total cost over 2 years (£)
Fixed wire testing	16,500	10,250	11,000
Installations	21,050	12,500	16,400
Load analysis	28,000	17,000	16,000

2a Based on an annual one year cost, which supplier provides the cheapest load analysis service?

A	B	C	D
Supplier 1	Supplier 2	Supplier 3	All the same

2b For the total cost for 3 years, which supplier provides the most expensive quote overall for fixed wire testing?

A	B	C	D
Supplier 1	Supplier 2	Supplier 3	All the same

2c Based on an annual one year cost and everything the supplier has to offer, which supplier is the most expensive?

A	B	C	D
Supplier 1	Supplier 2	Supplier 3	All the same

Sample Question 3

Below shows a list of quotes from three different suppliers. The quotes cover different periods of time. Theses quotes are for the cost of catering services.

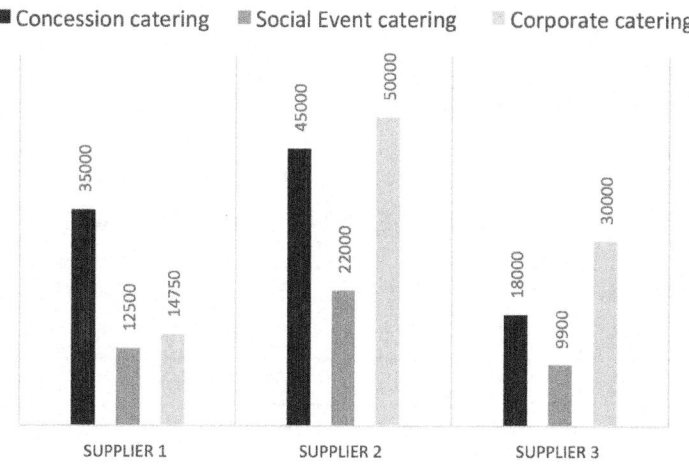

3a Based on an annual one year cost, which supplier provides the cheapest social event catering.

A	B	C	D
Supplier 1	Supplier 2	Supplier 3	All the same

3b What is the mean cost for all catering services from supplier 3, based on one year? To the nearest whole number.

A	B	C	D
6,430	6,433	6,323	6,343

3c Which supplier provides the most expensive corporate catering service, based on one year?

A	B	C	D
Supplier 1	Supplier 2	Supplier 2 & 3	All the same

Sample Question 4

Below are the test scores of 24 people. The test was a General Knowledge quiz. The test is marked out of 100.

64	53	19	75	33	51
46	87	47	49	91	90
26	18	55	50	64	76
14	49	62	80	80	65

4a What is the combined total of marks for all 24 people?

A	B	C	D
1,344	1,434	1,334	1,444

4b What was the mean score of all the results?

A	B	C	D
52	48	64	56

4c What percentage of the total number of people scored 50 or more in the General Knowledge quiz?

A	B	C	D
61.5%	50%	62.5%	60%

Answers

Sample Question 1 answers

1a. D (65)

Necklaces=12+ 42 + 32 + 4 + 6 = 96,

Watches= 3 + 11 + 10 + 8 + 2 =3 4,

Bracelets= 17 + 18 + 6 + 34 +3 2 = 107.

96+34+107=237 237 ÷ 365 (total number of items) x 100 = 64.931.

To the nearest whole number = 65

1b. A (106)

Necklaces = 12 + 42 + 32 + 4 + 6 + 24 + 36 = 156
Watches = 3 +11 + 10 + 8 + 2 + 4+ 12 = 50
150 − 50 = 106

1c. C (159:50)

Bracelets = 17 + 18 +6 + 34 + 32 + 12 + 40= 159
Watches = 3 + 11 + 10 + 8 + 2 + 4 + 12 = 50
So, the ratio of bracelets to watches = 159:50

Sample Question 2 answers

2a. A (Supplier 1)

Supplier 1; 28,000 ÷ 4 = 7,000.

Supplier 2; 17,000 ÷ 2 = 8,500.

Supplier 3; 16,000 ÷ 2 = 8,000.

2b. C (Supplier C)

Supplier 1; 16,500 ÷ 4 = 4,125 x 3 = 12,375.

Supplier 2; 10,250 ÷ 2 = 5,125 x 3 = 15,375.

Supplier 3; 11,000 ÷ 2 = 5,500 x 3 = 16,500.

2c. C (Supplier 3)

Supplier 1; 16,500 + 21,050 + 28,000 = 65,550 ÷ 4 = 16,387.50.

Supplier 2; 10,250 + 12,500 + 17,000 = 39,750 ÷ 2 = 19,875.

Supplier 3; 11,000 + 16,400 + 16,000 = 43,400 ÷ 2 = 21,700.

Sample Question 3 answers

3a. C (Supplier 3)

Supplier 1; £12,500 ÷ 2 = £6,250.

Supplier 2; £22,000 ÷ 5 = £4,400.

Supplier 3; £99,00 ÷ 3 = £3,300.

3b. B (6,433)

£18,000 + £9,900 + £30,000 = £57,900 ÷ 3 = £19,300

£19,300 ÷ 3 = £6,433.3

Rounded to 6,433.

3c. C (Suppliers 2 and 3)

.Supplier 1; £14,750 ÷ 2 = £7,375.

Supplier 2; £50,000 ÷ 5 = £10,000.

Supplier 3; £30,000 ÷ 3 = £10,000.

Sample Question 4 answers

4a. A (1,344)

Add up all of the test scores = 1,344

4b. D (56)

To work out the mean, add up all of the numbers, and then divide it by how many numbers there are.

1344 ÷ 24 = 56

4c. C (62.5%)

Out of the 24 people, 15 of them scored 50 or more marks in the test.

15 ÷ 24 x 100 = 62.5%

Civil Service
Numerical Reasoning
Test 2

In this practice test, you will be presented with a graph, table or chart and your task will be to analyse the graph/table/chart and answer questions based on the data.

Each practice exercise will have three questions that you will have to answer. In this test there are seven separate exercises each with 3 questions to answer. You may use a calculator if required.

You have 25 minutes to complete the 21 questions.

QUESTION 1

A Christmas bonus is being offered to the employee who secures the most number of sales across the next 20-day working period. The Christmas bonus will be an additional 20% of an employee's wages.

The table below shows the top six employees' sale results recorded weekly (5 working days).

NAME	TOM	DAVE	MARY	ALICIA	LOGAN	MILLIE
Week 1	3	4	0	3	4	6
Week 2	2	1	5	2	3	1
Week 3	4	6	2	4	4	5
Week 4	0	4	2	1	3	0

1. Which employee will receive the Christmas bonus?

A	B	C	D	E	F
Tom	Dave	Mary	Alicia	Logan	Millie

2. If the employee who receives the Christmas bonus earns £1,500 that month, what will their total wages be including the Christmas bonus?

A	B	C	D
£1,650	£1,800	£2,000	£2,200

3. What was the average number of sales across all six employees?

A	B	C	D
10	9.5	11.5	14

QUESTION 2

Below shows the earnings across different companies between the years 2010 to 2014.

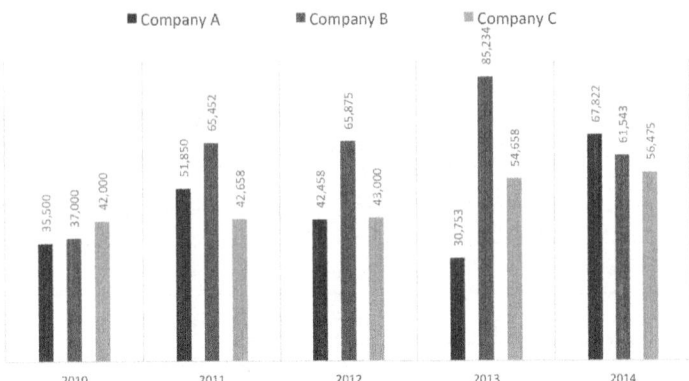

1. Work out the total earnings for Company B.

A	B	C	D
321,542	365,156	315,104	318,264

2. Which company had the greatest earnings between 2010 and 2014?

A	B	C	D
Company A	Company B	Company C	Company A and B

3. Work out the difference between the total earnings for Company B in 2010 compared to Company C in 2010.

A	B	C	D
3,000	4,500	4,000	5,000

QUESTION 3

Below is a field used for garden patches (indicated by the black rectangles). The diagram below shows how far apart each patch needs to be. The diagram is not drawn to scale and the lengths are shown in metres.

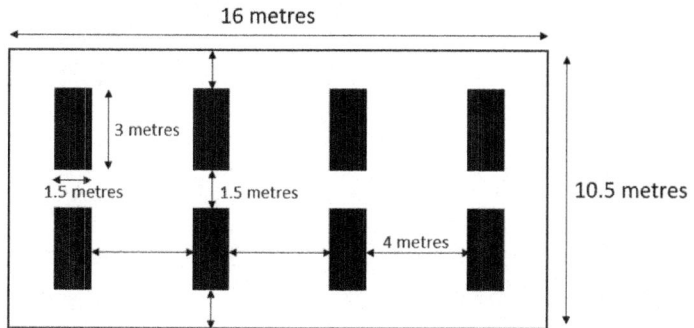

1. In square metres, what is the total area of the garden patches shown?.

A	B	C	D
36 sq m	18 sq m	8 sq m	42 sq m

2. Approximately, what percentage of the overall field is covered by garden patches?

A	B	C	D
20%	25%	21%	28%

3. Each garden patch requires full maintenance every 2 months. If maintenance costs £0.48 per square metre, work out the total cost for maintenance for the 8 garden patches.

A	B	C	D
£17.42	£16.58	£18.20	£17.28

QUESTION 4

Kent Police have put out a tender for car services and insurance. Below are quotes from 3 suppliers.

Charity event	Supplier 1 Total cost over 1 year (£)	Supplier 2 Total cost over 2 years (£)	Supplier 3 Total cost over 3 years (£)
Basic insurance	3,500	5,850	10,050
Insurance and breakdown cover	5,420	11,304	14,210
Insurance, breakdown cover and courtesy car	8,750	14,050	26,000

1. Which supplier provides the cheapest basic insurance, for one year?

A	B	C	D
Supplier 1	Supplier 2	Supplier 3	All the same

2. What percentage of the quote provided by Supplier 3 accounts for basic insurance? To 1 dp.

A	B	C	D
19%	19.1%	20%	20.1%

3. Over 5 years, how much would insurance, breakdown cover and courtesy car cost from supplier 1?

A	B	C	D
43,750	43,350	46,000	52,500

QUESTION 5

A performing arts school is made up of singers, dancers and actors. One third, or 105 students, are singers. There are twice as many dancers as there are actors.

1. In total, how many students attend the performing arts school?

A	B	C	D
250	315	412	219

2. What is the ratio of dancers to singers in the performing arts school?

A	B	C	D
2:1	5:4	4:3	3:2

3. In the following year, the number of dancers increases by 35%. Work out the total number of dancers in the following year.

A	B	C	D
203	176	195	189

QUESTION 6

There are two parts to your journey: for the first part, you travel 63 miles at a constant speed of 70 mph. You arrive at the service station at 13.21. You stay there for 15 minutes. You finish the second part of your journey at 14.53, travelling a total of 64 miles.

1. How long does the first part of your journey take?

A	B	C	D
36 minutes	1 hour and 10 minutes	1 hour and 8 minutes	54 minutes

2. What is the total duration of your journey, including the time spent at the service station?

A	B	C	D
2 hours, 26 minutes	2 hours, 22 minutes	2 hour, 3 minutes	2 hours, 11 minutes

3. What speed do you travel at for the second part of your journey?

A	B	C	D
50 mph	80 mph	55 mph	65 mph

QUESTION 7

The following table lists the type of bonus each member of staff will receive if they reach a specific number of sales per hour they work. The table has not yet been completed. Staff work seven hour shifts. In order to answer the questions, you will need to complete the table.

TIME	10 sales	20 sales	30 sales	40 sales
1st hour	£23.50	£27.50	£35.95	£42.60
2nd hour	£20.00	£23.50	-	£36.35
3rd hour	£16.50	-	£25.55	-
4th hour	£13.00	£15.50	£20.35	-
5th hour	£9.50	-	£15.15	£17.60
6th hour	-	£7.50	£9.95	£11.35
7th hour	£2.50	£3.50	-	£5.10

1. If the table was complete, how much could a worker earn in bonuses if they reached 10 sales every hour of their 7-hour shift?

A	B	C	D
£99.50	£101	£91.00	£98.50

2. How much would a worker earn in bonuses if they reached 20 sales per hour for the first 4 hours of their shift, and 40 sales per hour for the remaining 3 hours of their shift?

A	B	C	D
£120.05	£112.10	£120.50	£121.10

3. How much would a worker earn in bonuses if they reached 10 sales during their first and last hour, 20 sales during the 2nd and 6th hours, 30 sales during the 3rd and 5th hours, and 40 sales during the 4th hour?

A	B	C	D
£124.50	£124	£125.55	£121.55

ANSWERS AND EXPLANATIONS

Question 1

1. B = Dave

Tom = 9

Dave = 15

Mary = 9

Alicia = 10

Logan = 14

Millie = 12

2. B = £1,800

20% of £1,500 = 1,500 ÷ 100 x 120 = 1,800

3. C = 11.5

9 + 15 + 9 + 10 + 14 + 12 = 69

69 ÷ 6 = 11.5

Question 2

1. C = 315,104

37,000 + 65,452 + 65,875 + 85,234 + 61,543 = 315,104.

2. B = Company B

Company B = 315104. Company A = 228383. Company C = 238791.

3. D = 5,000

42,000 − 37,000 = 5,000.

Question 3

1. A = 36 sq m

The area of one garden patch = 3 x 1.5 = 4.5 sq m.
There are 8 garden patches in total = 4.5 x 8 = 36 sq m.

2. C = 21%

First of all, you need to work out the total area of the field = 16 x 10.5 = 168 square metres.

Using our answer to question 22, we know that the total area of garden patches is 36 square metres.

The percentage of garden patches in relation to the overall field = 36 ÷ 168 x 100 = 21.428...

To the nearest whole number = 21%

3. D = £17.28

We know that the total area of the garden patches is 36 square metres. That means the maintenance for all 8 patches would be = £0.48 x 36 = £17.28

Question 4

1. B = Supplier 2

Supplier 1; No calculation required as cost is already based on a single year.

Supplier 2; 5,850 ÷ 2 = 2,925.

Supplier 3; 10,050 ÷ 3 = 3,350.

2. C = 20%

10,050 + 14,210 + 26,000 = 50,260.

10,050 ÷ 50,260 x 100 = 19.99.

Rounded to 20%.

3. A = 43,750

8,750 x 5 = 43,750.

Question 5

1. B = 315

We know that 105 students make up one third of the school. That means there are 315 students in total (105 x 3).

2. C = 4:3

To work out the ratio, we need to work out the number of dancers. We know that there are twice as many dancers as there are actors.

315 − 105 = 210

That means there would be 140 dancers and 70 actors (210 ÷ 3 = 70) (70 x 2 = 140)

So the ratio of dancers to signers would be 140:105. In its simplest form, it would be 4:3

3. D = 189

The number of dancers was 140. If there was a 35% increase the following year, that means the number of dancers would be = 140 ÷ 100 x 135 = 189

Question 6

1. D = 54 minutes

63 (distance) ÷ 70 (speed) = 0.9 which is 54 minutes

2. A = 2 hour and 26 minutes

13:21 (arrive at service station) - 54 minutes (length of first part) = starting time of 12:27

14:53 (finish time) - 12:27 (start time) = 2 hours and 26 minutes

3. A = 50 mph

13:21 (arrive at service station) + 15 mins = 13:36

14:53 (finish time) - 13:36 = 1 hour and 17 minutes

64 (distance) / 1.28 (1 hour, 17 mins) = 50 mph

Question 7

1. C = £91

£23.50 + £20.00 + £16.50 + £13.00 + £9.50 + £6.00 + £2.50 = £91.00

2. A = £120.05

£27.50 + £23.50 + £19.50 + £15.50 = £86

£17.60 + £11.35 + £5.10 = £34.05

£86.00 + £34.05 = £120.05

3. D = £121.55

£23.50 + £2.50 + £23.50 + £7.50 + £25.55 + £15.15 + £23.85 = £121.55

Civil Service
Numerical Reasoning
Test 3

In this practice test, you will be presented with a graph, table or chart and your task will be to analyse the graph/table/chart and answer questions based on the data.

Each practice exercise will have three questions that you will have to answer. In this test there are seven separate exercises each with 3 questions to answer. You may use a calculator if required.

You have 25 minutes to complete the 21 questions.

QUESTION 1

Below is a chart which indicates the number of sick days taken per quarter at the Arlingford Car Depot.

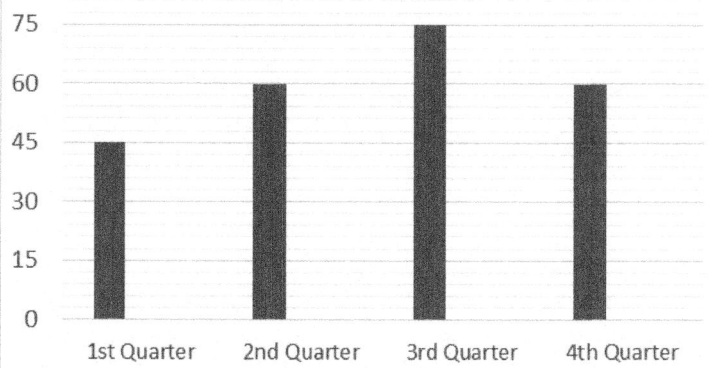

1. How many days sickness was taken in total during the year?

A	B	C	D
220	200	240	120

2. What was the average number of days sickness taken per quarter?

A	B	C	D
40	50	60	80

3. If the total number of sickness days reduced the following year by 40%, what would the total be for that year?

A	B	C	D
144	96	80	190

QUESTION 2

The following graph indicates the total monthly profits of three competing companies during a 5-month period.

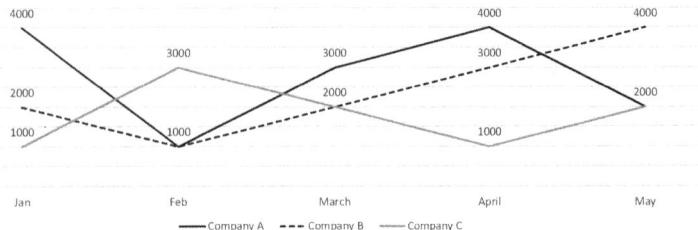

1. Over the 5-month period, which company(s) made the greatest profit?

A	B	C	D
Company A	Company B	Company C	Companies A and B

2. What were the total combined profits for all three companies over the 5-month period?

A	B	C	D
25,000	35,000	27,000	32,000

3. During which month was the average profit across the three companies the lowest?

A	B	C	D	E
January	February	March	April	May

QUESTION 3

The pie chart below shows the percentage of students in each faculty at Grove University, and the number of Non-US students in the Business faculty. These percentages have been rounded to the nearest whole number.

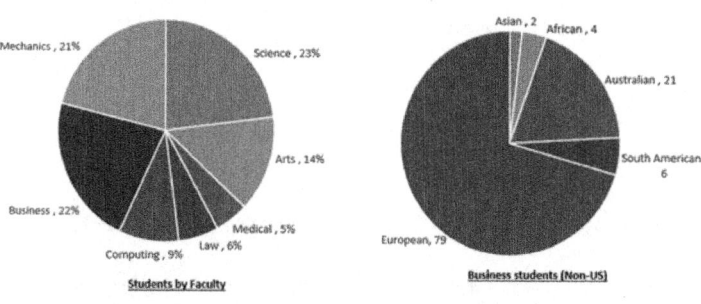

There is a total of 1,247 students in the Business faculty.

1. What percentage of students in the Business faculty are Non-US students?

A	B	C	D
11%	13%	9%	7%

2. How many students are there at the university?

A	B	C	D
5,558	5,668	5,685	55,85

3. How many students are there studying Law?

A	B	C	D
310	290	380	340

QUESTION 4

Kent Police have put out a tender for heating maintenance and installation. Below are quotes from 3 suppliers.

Heating maintenance and installation	Supplier 1 Total cost over 3 years (£)	Supplier 2 Total cost over 2 years (£)	Supplier 3 Total cost over 5 years (£)
Installation and boiler replacements	24,630	19,750	36,150
Hot Air Systems	142,530	102,640	229,850
Service and maintenance	17,880	12,460	25,625

1. Amongst all three suppliers, based on an annual cost, what is the average cost to install hot air systems?

A	B	C	D
45,804	50,000	48,266	47,655

2. Based on 2 years, what supplier provides the most expensive quote for installation and boiler replacements?

A	B	C	D
Supplier 1	Supplier 2	Supplier 3	Supplier 1 and 3

3. What percentage of the total quote provided by Supplier 2 accounts for hot air systems?

A	B	C	D
75%	76.1%	77.4%	73.9%

QUESTION 5

Katie and Harrison take a road trip. There are two parts of the journey in which they decide to split the driving. For the first part of the journey, Katie drives 90 miles at an average speed of 60 mph. They stop off at a petrol station for 20 minutes, before Harrison takes over the next part of the journey. They leave the petrol station at 1355 and arrive at their destination at 1525, travelling a distance of 60 miles.

1. How long does the first part of the journey take?

A	B	C	D
1 hour and 30 minutes	1 hour	2 hours	2 hours and 15 minutes

2. What is the duration of the whole journey, including the stop off?

A	B	C	D
4 hours	3 hours and 20 minutes	3 hours and 45 minutes	4 hours and 15 minutes

3. What speed do you travel at for the second part of the journey?

A	B	C	D
30 mph	35 mph	40 mph	45 mph

QUESTION 6

Below is a list of percentage changes from 2012 to 2014 for five different companies.

Company	% change from 2012 – 2013	% change from 2013 – 2014
Company A	+17%	-5%
Company B	+12%	+5%
Company C	-11%	+8%
Company D	-5%	-7%
Company E	+8%	-3%

1. At Company E, the amount of sales for 2013 was what percentage of the amount of sales for 2014? To 1 decimal place.

A	B	C	D
3.1%	97.3%	103.1%	115.9%

2. If Company B earned £412,500 in 2012, how much did they earn in 2014?

A	B	C	D
£316,875	£462,000	£415,290	£485,100

3. If Company C earned £300,00 in 2013, how much did they earn in 2014?

A	B	C	D
£324,000	£314,000	£350,000	£304,000

QUESTION 7

Below is a list of the marks scored by 100 students.

Subject	Marks out of 40			
	30 and above	20 and above	10 and above	0 and above
English	19	52	91	100
Maths	13	36	90	100
Science	11	42	87	100
Average	11	43	89	100

1. How many people scored 20 and above in their Maths exam?

A	B	C	D
52	43	36	42

2. What is the percentage of students who achieved marks of 20 or above in their English exam?

A	B	C	D
26%	41%	56%	52%

3. What is the difference between the number of students who achieved 30 or above in English and the number of students who achieved 20 and above in Science?

A	B	C	D
23	25	27	31

ANSWERS AND EXPLANATIONS

Question 1

1. C = 240

45 + 60 + 75 + 60 = 240

2. C = 60

240 ÷ 4 = 60

3. A = 144

240 ÷ 100 x 60 = 144

Question 2

1. A = Company A

Company A made a profit of 14,000

Company B made a profit of 12,000

Company C made a profit of 9,000

Therefore, Company A made the largest profit.

2. B = 35,000

14,000 + 12,000 + 9,000 = 35,000

3. B = February

You need to work out the average profit across all three companies for each month:

January = 4,000 + 2,000 + 1,000 = 7,000
7,000 ÷ 3 = 2,333

February = 3,000 + 1,000 + 1,000 = 5,000
5,000 ÷ 3 = 1,666

March = 3,000 + 2,000 + 2,000 = 7,000
7,000 ÷ 3 = 2,333

April = 4,000 + 3,000 + 1,000 = 8,000
8,000 ÷ 3 = 2,666

May = 4,000 + 2,000 + 2,000 = 8,000
8,000 ÷ 3 = 2,666

Therefore, February had the lowest average profit across all three companies.

Question 3

1. C = 9%

112 ÷ 1,247 x 100 = 8.98. Rounded to the nearest whole number = 9%.

2. B = 5,668

1,247 x 100 ÷ 22 = 5,668

3. D = 340

5,668 ÷ 100 x 6 = 340

Question 4

1. C = 48,266

2. B = Supplier 2

3. B = 76.1

Question 5

1. A = 1 hour and 30 minutes
2. B = 3 hours and 20 minutes
3. C = 40 mph

Question 6

1. C = 103.1%

If A is the amount of sales at Company E for 2013, then 3 percent of A, or 0.03 , A is the amount of decrease from 2013 to 2014. Thus 0.03 = 0.97 (to make a whole one).

Therefore, the desired percent can be obtained by dividing A by 0.97. So, 1 ÷ 0.97 = 1.0309 x 100 = 103.09. Expressed as a percentage to the nearest tenth = 103.1%.

2. D = £485,100

412,500 ÷ 100 x 112 = 462,000. From 2013 to 2014, the company saw a 5% increase, which is 105% of the previous month.

So, 462,000 ÷ 100 x 105 = 485,100. So, the correct answer is £485,100.

3. A = £324,000

£300,000 ÷ 100 x 108 = £324,000

Question 7

1. C = 36

36 students scored 20 and above.

2. D = 52%

52% of students scored 20 or above in their English exam.

3. A = 23

42 − 19 = 23

Verbal Reasoning Test

What is a Verbal Reasoning Test?

A verbal reasoning test (VRT) is a form of psychometric test which assesses candidate's ability to understand various written passages. A verbal reasoning test can come in a wide range of different formats, such as, odd one out, missing words, jumbled words, missing letter, moving letters and many more. However, the form of verbal reasoning test you will have to undertake as part of your Civil Service assessment is a test known as True, False or Cannot Say. This form of verbal reasoning test has been used widelymany organisations worldwide for a number of years now. A basic overview of the True, False or Cannot say question, will include a passage of text or scenario.

Choosing Your Answers

Using only the information in the text, you will have to answer questions, deciding on whether the question is a true or false reflection of what is stated in the passage. Alternatively, you may be unable to confirm that statement as true or false. In these instances the correct answer will be 'cannot say' as the statement cannot be confirmed as explicitly true or false.you will have three choices to choose from for each question. True, False or Cannot Say.

Although this seems quite straightforward, it's easy to get caught out! Many people will inadvertently answer using information they know to be true in reality. For example, it may be law that you have to be 21 or over to drink alcohol in your country, but if this is not mentioned in the scenario or passage that you are presented with then you cannot base your answers on this knowledge. In other words, your answer choices must be based solely on what is written in the passage, and not what you know to be true.

A Sample Civil Service Verbal Question, Answers & Explanations

Below is a sample question showing the typical type of passage and questions you can except to face during your Civil Service verbal reasoning test.

Sample Question Scenario:

There is a minimum right to paid holiday, but your employer may offer more than this. All employees are entitled to a minimum of 5.6 weeks paid leave per year. Those employees who work for five days a week are entitled to 28 days per year annual leave (capped at a statutory maximum of 28 days for all working patterns). Employees who work part-time are entitled to the same level of holiday pro rata (5.6 times your normal working week) e.g. 16.8 days for someone working three days a week. All employees will start building up holiday entitlement as soon as they start work with the employer.

The employer has the right to control when you take your holiday but you must get paid the same level of pay whilst on holiday. When you finish working for an employer you get paid for any holiday you have not taken. The employer may include bank and public holidays in your minimum entitlement.

You continue to be entitled to your holiday leave throughout any additional maternity/paternity leave and adoption leave.

Verbal Reasoning Test

Take a look at the questions below, and answer them with either TRUE, FALSE OR CANNOT SAY.

1. *An employer may not offer you more than the minimum paid holiday.*

2. *In addition to paternity leave you are entitled to your normal holiday.*

3. *All employees only start building up holiday leave 5.6 weeks after commencement of employment.*

4. *Employees who receive more than the minimum holiday entitlement are often grateful to their employer.*

Answers

Write your answers to each of the questions below selecting only true, false, or cannot say.

1.

2.

3.

4.

Answers and Explanations to the Sample Question

1. An employer may not offer you more than the minimum paid holiday.

By reading the passage carefully you will note that the following sentence relates to Question 1:

"There is a minimum right to paid holiday, but your employer may offer more than this."

We can deduce from the passage that Question 1 is in fact false, simply because an employer may offer more than the minimum paid holiday.

Fortunately for us the first question related to the very first sentence in the passage. However, in the majority of cases this will not be the norm.

2. In addition to paternity leave you are entitled to your normal holiday.

By reading the passage carefully you will note that the following sentence relates to Question 2:

"You continue to be entitled to your holiday leave throughout any additional maternity/paternity leave and adoption leave."

We can deduce from the passage that Question 2 is in fact true. An employee is entitled to their holiday leave throughout paternity leave.

3. All employees only start building up holiday leave 5.6 weeks after commencement of employment.

By reading the passage carefully you will note that the following sentence relates to Question 3:

"All employees will start building up holiday as soon as they start work with the employer."

We can deduce from the passage that Question 3 is in fact false based on the information provided. An employee starts building up holiday as soon as they start work with the employer, not 5.6 weeks after commencement of employment.

4. Employees who receive more than the minimum holiday entitlement are often grateful to their employer.

By reading the passage carefully you will note that none of the content relates to the question. At no point does it state that employees who receive more than the minimum holiday entitlement are often grateful to their employer, or otherwise. Therefore, the answer is cannot say based on the information provided. Although it is probably true in real life that most employees would be grateful for receiving more than the minimum holiday requirement, we can only answer the question based solely on the information provided in the passage.

●

The Civil Service Verbal Test Structure

As previously explored the Civil Service Verbal Test is a format where you have to read a passage or scenario and answer questions based on the passage. There are three ways you can answer each of the questions. If you believe the question to be a true reflection of what is written in the passage, then answer the question as true. If you believe that the answer is not a true reflection of the passage, then you would choose false as your answer. The last choice cannot say, is suitable for scenario's where you are unable to determine from the statement if the answer is true or false.

The test itself is not timed so you can afford to allocate as much time as possible or as required for each of the questions. It is important to note that with the verbal test, if you get a question right the difficulty will increase on the next question. However if you get a question wrong the difficulty will decrease on the following question.

When deciding to take the test it is vital that you will be in a comfortable environment where you will not be disturbed by others. Planning the time to do the test is very important, so try to bear in mind the following:

- Find a well-lit and quiet area, where you can sit comfortably to undertake the test using a PC or laptop.

- Allocate a time to do the test, when you are unlikely to be disturbed by others in your household.

- Plan to take the test when you are most mentally active. Do not take the test when you are most fatigued at the end of the day or under the influence of alcohol.

- Ensure you stay hydrated and eat a healthy meal prior to taking your test, this will aid your concentration levels.

- Ensure your internet connection is stable, the last thing you want is to lose your internet connection half way through your test.

- Allocate plenty of time to complete the test, if you think it will take an hour, allocate two hours. Remember the test is not timed, so there is no need to rush.

Taking the Civil Service Verbal Test

Once you have received your invitation, plan to undertake the test as soon as possible to avoid missing the deadline for completion.

Remember the test is not timed so you can allow to take your time and not rush. Also as stated previously the question difficulty will increase/decrease dependent on the answers previously submitted. If you answered correctly the difficulty will increase. If you answered incorrectly the difficulty will decrease.

One of the most important things to remember is this. If it is not written in the scenario, and even if you know to be true in reality, this must be discounted. You must always base your answer on the statement and nothing more. Another tip worth noting is this. Pay attention to the small words such as 'may' or 'had'. For example, the passage/scenario may state, 'The witness said the person may have had blue trousers on'. If the question states the following 'The person may have had blue trousers on'. You would answer this as **true**. However, If the question states 'the person had blue trousers on' you should answer this as **cannot say** as you cannot categorically state this from the information contained within the passage/scenario. So always pay attention to the smallest of details.

Sample CSVT Question

People pay National Insurance contributions in order to build up their entitlement to a state pension and other social security benefits.

The amount that you pay is directly linked to the amount you earn. If you earn over a certain amount, your employer deducts Class 1 National Insurance contributions from your wages through the PAYE system.

You pay a lower rate of National Insurance contributions if you're a member of your employer's 'contracted' pension scheme, or you're a married woman – or widow – who holds a valid 'election certificate'.

Your employer also pays employer National Insurance contributions based on your earnings and on any benefits you get with your job, for example a company car. HMRC keeps track of your contributions through your National Insurance number. This is like an account number and is unique to you.

1. People pay National Insurance contributions in order to build up housing benefits? How would you answer this question, please choose one of the options below.

- True

- False
- Cannot Say

2. HMRC stands for 'Her Majesty's Revenue and Customs'?

- True
- False
- Cannot Say

3. An employer pays employer National Insurance contributions if an employee has a company car.

- True
- False
- Cannot Say

Please see the suggested answers and explanations for this example questions below.

Sample CSVT Answer and Explanation

1. People pay National Insurance contributions in order to build up housing benefits?

Answer: Cannot Say

Explanation: Although the statement makes reference to social security benefits, it does not confirm that these include housing benefits. The correct answer is cannot say based on the information provided.

2. HMRC stands for 'Her Majesty's Revenue and Customs'?

Answer: Cannot Say

Explanation: The passage makes no reference to this fact; therefore, the correct answer is cannot say based on the information provided. Also, this is a perfect example of where we must discount information that we know to be true in reality, but is not referred to in the passage.

3. An employer pays employer National Insurance contributions if an employee has a company car.

Answer: True

Explanation: The passage states that "Your employer also pays employer National Insurance contributions based on your earnings and on any benefits you get with your job, for example a company car". The statement is true.

Scoring of the Test and Your Results

Upon completion of your test you will advised of your results, but not if you have passed or not.

The tests are scored dependent on the number of questions faced and also the difficulty of the test questions faced. Your score will then be compared to other candidates who have taken the same test. When you do receive your results, you will receive these as a percentile. This is not a percentage of questions answered correctly. This is based on your performance compared to the other candidates. For example, if you scored a percentile of 62%, this means that you scored higher than 62% of the other candidates.

All of the roles within the Civil Service are advertised to a certain level. If you have been successful at passing the minimum standard for the level of the role applying for, a number of things may happen. If the role you are applying for requires further tests, you will be sent an invitation to complete the further tests. After the deadline for the test has passed, the assessors will look at all of the candidates scores and will decide upon this what the roles pass mark will be.

After evaluating all results, the assessors can raise the pass mark, but this is generally dependent on the number of candidates amassing the passing score. If the assessors do decide to raise the score, you will be informed of this and if you have passed or not at the raised standard.

If at this time your application is not successful, but your test score has reached the minimum standard your score will be banked for 6 months and if you apply for roles of the same grade within the time frame, you will not have to resit the test.

Civil Service Verbal Reasoning Test 1

For the following 18 questions, please read each scenario/passage and answer each following question either true, false or cannot Say.

Sample Passage 1 - Long Service Payments.

Employees who attain fifteen years' continuous service between 7th November 2003 and 30th June 2007 shall qualify for the long-service payment at the rate applicable at the time. Employees who are promoted to a higher role during this period will cease to qualify for the payment but will receive a minimum pay increase on promotion of £300 per annum, which will be achieved through partial protection of the long-service payment.

Where the pay assimilation process on 7th November 2003 created a basic pay increase of more than 7%, and the employee was in receipt of the long-service payment, the payment has been reduced with effect from that date by the amount that the increase exceeded 7%. The consequent pay rates were set out in circular NJC/01/04.

PAY PROTECTION FOR EMPLOYEES ON THE RETAINED DUTY SYSTEM
Where an employee on the retained duty system has not received a pay increase of at least 7% (for the same pattern and level of activity) following full implementation of the pay award effective from 7th November 2003, the fire and rescue authority may introduce arrangements to ensure that such an increase is achieved.

1. If an employee who is on the retained duty system has not received a pay increase of at least 7% following the implementation of the pay award, the fire and rescue service must introduce arrangements to ensure that such an increase is achieved.

True	False	Cannot Say

2. Employees who attain fifteen years' continuous service between 7th November 2003 and 30th June 2008 shall qualify for the long-service payment at the rate applicable at the time.

True	False	Cannot Say

3. The pay assimilation process on 7th November 2003 created a basic pay increase for all employees of more than 7%.

True	False	Cannot Say

Sample Passage 2 - Magistrate Training.

The entire selection process for becoming a magistrate can take approximately 12 months, sometimes longer depending on the area.

Once you have been accepted you will be required to undertake a comprehensive training course which is usually held over a 3-day period (18 hours). During this course you will learn the necessary skills that are required in order to become a magistrate.

The training is normally carried out by the Justice Clerk who is responsible for the court. He/she will usually be the legal advisor during your magistrate sittings. They will help you to develop all the necessary skills required in order to carry out your duties professionally and competently.

You will carry out your training as part of a group with other people who have been recruited at the same time as you. This is extremely beneficial as it will allow you to learn in a safe environment.

Training will be given using a variety of methods, which may include pre-course reading, small-group work, use of case studies, computer-based training and CCTV. It is recognised that magistrates are volunteers and that their time is valuable, so every effort is made to provide all training at times and places convenient to trainees. The Ministry of Justice booklet 'Serving as a Magistrate' has more information about the magistracy and the role of magistrates.

4. The comprehensive training course for becoming a magistrate usually consists of 3 days, divided into 6 hours training per day.

True	False	Cannot Say

5. An applicant can find out more about the role of a magistrate by reading the Ministry of Justice booklet 'Serving as a Magistrate'.

True	False	Cannot Say

6. The selection process for becoming a magistrate will take no longer than 12 months.

True	False	Cannot Say

Sample Passage 3 - The Role of the Ambulance Service.

Most people believe that the Ambulance Service is simply there to respond to emergency incidents such as road traffic collisions (RTCs), seriously ill or injured patients, fires and other such incidents. While these are the core roles that the service undertakes, there are also a number of other important duties that are carried out, such as patient transport services.

The latter is carried out by the employees of the Ambulance Service, who carry disabled, elderly and vulnerable people to and from out-patient appointments, hospital admissions and also to and from day centres and clinics. Behind the operational ambulance crew is a team of people who have different roles, all designed to provide the necessary support required that is so valued by the community.

To begin with, there are the 999 call operators who take the initial calls. Their job is to gather as much information as possible about the emergency call, the nature of the incident, its location and the level of response that is required.

These people are integral to the Ambulance Service and are crucial to patient care. For example, if a patient is critically ill they may need to talk the caller through a life-saving procedure while they wait for the ambulance crews to get there.

7. The 999 call operators do not travel in the ambulance with the paramedics.

True	False	Cannot Say

8. Responding to road traffic collisions forms part of the core role of the Ambulance Service.

True	False	Cannot Say

9. 999 call operators may need to talk the caller through a life-saving procedure while they wait for the ambulance crews to get there.

True	False	Cannot Say

Sample Passage 4 - Business Franchise Information.

Franchises are very popular at the moment with increasing numbers of people choosing to buy one as opposed to starting out by setting up their own business. By purchasing a franchise you are effectively taking advantage of the success of an already established business. As the 'franchisee', you are buying a license to use the name, products, services, and management support systems of the "franchiser" company. This license normally covers a particular geographical area and runs for a limited time. The downside to a franchise is that you will never actually legally own the business.

As a franchisee, the way you pay for the franchise may be through an initial fee, ongoing management fees, a share of your turnover, or a combination of these depending on how you have set up the franchise. A franchise business can take different legal forms - most are sole traders, partnerships or limited companies. Whatever the structure, the franchisee's freedom to manage the business is limited by the terms of the franchise agreement.

There is information to suggest that the franchise business sector is still growing rapidly. During 2007 the Lionhahare Bank carried out a survey into the UK franchise market which revealed the astonishing financial growth of this sector. The approximate annual turnover of the business franchise sector is in excess of £10.8 billion.

What is more interesting to note is that the vast majority of business franchisees in 2007 were in profit - a total of 93% to be exact. In 1991 the total number of profitable franchisees was 70% and in 2004 it was 88%. Therefore, this business sector is growing.

10. During 2007 the total number of business franchises that were not in profit totalled 7%.

True	False	Cannot Say

11. As the 'franchiser', you are buying a licence to use the name, products, services, and management support systems of the 'franchisee' company.

True	False	Cannot Say

12. A franchise business can take different legal forms including Limited Liability Partnership (LLP).

True	False	Cannot Say

Sample Passage 5 - Central Heating System.

Over half the money spent on fuel bills in the UK goes towards providing heating and hot water. Therefore, having an efficient boiler and central heating system is crucial to helping you to reduce costs. If your boiler and central heating system are in a poor state of repair, this can add up to an extra third on your heating bills.

In order to save money on your heating bills you must first of all under- stand your current system. The vast majority of homes in the UK have either a central heating system, consisting of a boiler and radiators, or they use electric storage heaters. This is the most common form of heating in the UK. A single boiler heats up water that is pumped through pipes to radiators throughout the house as well as providing hot water for the kitchen and bathroom taps.

Gas, oil and LPG boilers may be combination boilers, in which case they heat the hot water as it is needed and don't need to store it. Otherwise, the boiler heats up water and it is stored in a hot water cylinder that then feeds the taps. If you have a system like this, your options for energy-saving improvements include:

- Replacing your current boiler with a more modern/efficient model.
- Fitting better controls to your system.
- Using the controls on your current system to only generate heat where and when you want it.

- Switching to a cheaper or lower carbon fuel or technology such as wood-fuelled or solar water heating.
- Making any insulation and draught-proofing improvements that you can.

13. Most people in the UK are concerned about rising fuel bills.

True	False	Cannot Say

14. If your boiler and central heating system are in a poor state of repair, this can add over an extra third on your heating bills.

True	False	Cannot Say

15. If you have a combination boiler system, one of your options for energy-saving improvements is fitting better controls to your system.

True	False	Cannot Say

Sample Passage 6 - Company Ordering Process.

1.1 Our display of products and online services on our website is an invitation and not an offer to sell those goods to you.

1.2 An offer is made when you place the order for your products or online service. However, we will not have made a contract with you unless and until we accept your offer.

1.3 We take payment from your card when we process your order and have checked your card details. Goods are subject to availability. If we are unable to supply the goods, we will inform you of this as soon as possible. A full refund will be given if you have already paid for the goods. It is our aim to always keep our website updated and all goods displayed available.

1.4 If you enter a correct email address we will send you an order acknowledgement email immediately and receipt of payment. These do not constitute an order confirmation or order acceptance from us.

1.5 Unless we have notified you that we do not accept your order or you have cancelled it, order acceptance and the creation of the contract between you and us will take place at the point the goods you have ordered are dispatched.

1.6 The contract will be formed at the place of dispatch of the goods. All goods, wherever possible, will be dispatched within 24 hours of the order being placed, Monday to Thursday. If your order falls on a weekend or bank holiday, your order will be dispatched on the next available working day. All orders that are sent via recorded delivery will require a signature. In the majority of cases, however, we will dispatch goods using Royal Mail's standard First Class delivery service.

16. If a customer places an order, and they have entered a correct email address, they will immediately receive an order confirmation email.

True	False	Cannot Say

17. Orders placed on a Friday will be dispatched on a Saturday.

True	False	Cannot Say

18. Payment is taken from the card once the card details have been checked.

True	False	Cannot Say

Answers

Sample Passage 1 Answers:

1. If an employee who is on the retained duty system has not received a pay increase of at least 7% following the implementation of the pay award, the fire and rescue service must introduce arrangements to ensure that such an increase is achieved.

Answer: False

Explanation: This statement is false because the sentence states that the fire and rescue service 'may' introduce arrangements; it does not say they 'must'.

2. Employees who attain fifteen years' continuous service between 7th November 2003 and 30th June 2008 shall qualify for the long-service payment at the rate applicable at the time.

Answer: False

Explanation: This statement is false because the sentence states 30th June 2008, instead of 30th June 2007 as stated in the passage.

3. The pay assimilation process on 7th November 2003 created a basic pay increase for all employees of more than 7%.'

Answer: Cannot Say

Explanation: We cannot say that this statement is true or false. It makes no reference in the passage that 'all' employees received a pay rise.

Sample Passage 2 Answers:

4. The comprehensive training course for becoming a magistrate usually consists of 3 days, divided into 6 hours training per day.

Answer: Cannot Say

Explanation: The passage does state that the training course is usually held over a 3-day period (18 hours). We could assume that the 18 hours are equally divided into 3 × 6 hour days. However, it is not our job to assume; we must base our answers on what is provided within the passage. Therefore, the correct answer is cannot say.

5. An applicant can find out more about the role of a magistrate by reading the Ministry of Justice booklet 'Serving as a Magistrate'.

Answer: True

Explanation: From the passage we know this statement to be true.

6. The selection process for becoming a magistrate will take no longer than 12 months.

Answer: False

Explanation: This statement is false because the passage states that the selection process can sometimes take longer than 12 months.

Sample Passage 3 Answers:

7. The 999 call operators do not travel in the ambulance with the paramedics.

Answer: Cannot Say

Explanation: The passage makes no reference to this statement. The correct answer is cannot say from the information provided.

8. Responding to road traffic collisions forms part of the core role of the Ambulance Service.

Answer: True

Explanation: The passage makes it clear that responding to road traffic collisions is a core role for the Ambulance Service. The statement is true.

9. 999 call operators may need to talk the caller through a life-saving procedure while they wait for the ambulance crews to get there.

Answer: True

Explanation: From the passage we can confirm that this statement is true.

Sample Passage 4 Answers:

10. During 2007 the total number of business franchises that were not in profit totalled 7%.

Answer: True

Explanation: The passage states that 93% of business franchises in 2007 were in profit. This means that 7% were not in profit. The correct answer is true.

11. As the 'franchiser', you are buying a licence to use the name, products, services, and management support systems of the 'franchisee' company.

Answer: False

Explanation: The passage states "As the 'franchisee', you are buying a licence to use the name, products, services, and management support systems of the 'franchiser' company". The correct answer is false.

12. A franchise business can take different legal forms including Limited Liability Partnership (LLP).

Answer: Cannot Say

Explanation: We cannot state whether this sentence is true or false from the information provided. The passage states only that "a franchise business can take different legal forms". We cannot assume that this includes Limited Liability Partnerships (LLP). The correct answer is cannot say.

Sample Passage 5 Answers:

13. Most people in the UK are concerned about rising fuel bills.

Answer: Cannot say

Explanation: The passage does make reference to heating bills but not in respect of the statement. The answer is cannot say based on the information provided.

14. If your boiler and central heating system are in a poor state of repair, this can add over an extra third on your heating bills.

Answer: False

Explanation: The passage states "If your boiler and central heating system are in a poor state of repair, this can add up to an extra third on your heating bills." Because the statement refers to it adding over an extra third on your heating bills the correct answer is false.

15. If you have a combination boiler system, one of your options for energy-saving improvements is fitting better controls to your system.

Answer: Cannot Say

Explanation: In respect of energy saving improvements and fitting netter controls to your system, the passage is referring to systems where the water is stored in a hot water cylinder. We cannot tell from the information in the passage if the same applies to combination boiler systems. Therefore, the correct answer is cannot say.

Sample Passage 6 Answers:

16. If a customer places an order, and they have entered a correct email address, they will immediately receive an order confirmation email.

Answer: False

Explanation: The passage states that if a correct email address is entered they will send the customer an order acknowledgment email. It goes on to state that this email is not an order confirmation. The correct answer is false.

17. Orders placed on a Friday will be dispatched on a Saturday.

Answer: Cannot Say

Explanation: The passage states "If your order falls on a weekend or bank holiday, your order will be dispatched on the next available working day". Although we could assume that the next 'working day' is Monday, this cannot be confirmed by the text in the passage. It could quite possibly be that the company classes Saturday as a working day. Therefore, the correct answer is cannot say based on the information provided.

18. Payment is taken from the card once the card details have been checked.

Answer: True

Explanation: From the information provided in the passage we can confirm that this sentence is true.

Civil Service Verbal Reasoning Test 2

The following 21 questions are split evenly between 7 sample passages in banks of 3 questions per passage. Your task is to answer each question either true, false or cannot say.

Civil Service Verbal Reasoning Test 2

Here's a quick reminder of what is meant by TRUE, FALSE or CANNOT SAY, in the context of a verbal reasoning test.

TRUE - If a statement is 'true', then it can be verified by the text. This means that the text must explicitly or implicitly mention something which proves the statement to be correct. In other words, you cannot make any assumptions about the text. There must either be direct evidence for the statement, or a strong inference to support the statement.

FALSE - If a statement is 'false', there must be evidence in the text which contradicts the statement. For example, if the question statement says 'all swans are white', but the text says 'there is such a thing as a black swan', then the statement is false because it is directly contradicted by the text.

CANNOT SAY - If there is not enough evidence to verify that the statement is true or false, then the correct answer is 'cannot say' Simply put, this means that you cannot say the statement is true or false based on the information provided in the passage.

PASSAGE 1 – WINTER FUEL PAYMENTS

Members of the public may get a winter Fuel Payment if they have reached the qualifying age (born on or before 5 January 1951) and they also normally live in Great Britain or Northern Ireland on any day in the week of 19–25 September 2011. They won't qualify for a Winter Fuel Payment if, throughout the week of 19–25 September 2011, they were in hospital or a care home for more than 52 weeks previously, getting free treatment as an in-patient.

They will also not qualify if they were in custody serving a court sentence, were subject to immigration control and did not qualify for help from the Department for work and Pensions, lived in a care home, an independent hospital, received income-based Jobseeker's Allowance or income-related Employment and Support Allowance.

In addition to these restrictions you cannot qualify for a Winter Fuel Payment if you move to another European Economic Area country or Switzerland.

Winter Fuel Payment is paid for the household and will be paid directly into your bank account or by cheque depending on which format you requested.

QUESTION 1 - You can qualify for a Winter Fuel Payment if you move to France.

True	False	Cannot Say

QUESTION 2 - Winter Fuel Payment can only be paid directly in your bank account.

True	False	Cannot Say

QUESTION 3 - Members of the public will not qualify for a Winter Fuel Payment if, throughout the week of 19–25 September 2011, they were in a care home.

True	False	Cannot Say

PASSAGE 2 – WHITEHAM SUPERMARKET

Barry and Bill work at their local supermarket in the town of Whiteham. Barry works every day except Wednesday.

The supermarket is run by Barry's brother Elliot who is married to Sarah. Sarah and Elliot have two children called Marcus and Michelle who are both seven- years-old and they live in the road adjacent to the supermarket.

Barry lives in a town called Redford, which is seven miles from Whiteham. Bill's girlfriend, Maria, works in a factory in her hometown of Brownhaven.

The town of Redford is four miles from Whiteham and six miles from the seaside town of Tenford. Sarah and Elliot take their children on holiday to Tenford twice a year and Barry usually gives them a lift in his car. Barry's mum lives in Tenford and he tries to visit her once a week at 2pm when he is not working.

QUESTION 4 - Brownhaven is seven miles from Whiteham.

True	False	Cannot Say

QUESTION 5 – Barry works at the local supermarket on Sundays.

True	False	Cannot Say

QUESTION 6 – The town of Redford is four miles from the town of Tenford.

True	False	Cannot Say

PASSAGE 3 – FAMILY HOLIDAY

Janet and Steve have been married for twenty-seven years. They have a daughter called Jessica who is twenty-five-years-old. They all want to go on holiday together but cannot make up their minds on where to go.

Janet's first choice would be somewhere hot and sunny abroad. Her second choice would be somewhere in their home country that involves a sporting activity. She does not like hill-climbing or walking holidays but her third choice would be a skiing holiday.

Steve's first choice would be a walking holiday in the hills somewhere in their home country and his second choice would be a sunny holiday abroad. He does not enjoy skiing. Jessica's first choice would be a skiing holiday and her second choice would be a sunny holiday abroad. Jessica's third choice would be a walking holiday in the hills of their home country.

QUESTION 7 - Jessica's first choice would be a walking holiday in the hills of their home country.

True	False	Cannot Say

QUESTION 8 – Janet and Jessica have been married for twenty-seven years.

True	False	Cannot Say

QUESTION 9 – Jessica would rather go skiing than go on a sunny holiday abroad.

True	False	Cannot Say

PASSAGE 4 – DATA WAREHOUSES

A data warehouse is the main source of information for an organisation's historical data. Its historical data is often referred to as its corporate memory. As an example of how a data warehouse can be put to good use, an organisation would use the information stored in its data warehouse to find out how many particular stock items they sold on a particular day in a particular year. They could also ascertain which employees were off sick on any given day or any given year. The data stored within the warehouse contains essential information so that managers can make appropriate management decisions.

A data warehouse is normally large in size as the information stored usually focuses on basic, structured and organised data. Some of the characteristics of the data in a data warehouse are as follows:

Time-variant - changes to the data in the database are tracked and recorded so that reports can be produced showing changes over time;

Non-volatile - the data in the database is never over-written or deleted but is retained for future reporting;

Integrated - the database contains data from most or all of an organisation's operational applications. This data is useful and meaningful for further processing and analysis.

QUESTION 10 - Integrated and non-volatile data form some of the characteristics of a data warehouse.

True	False	Cannot Say

QUESTION 11 – It is not possible to identify which employees were on sick leave from the information stored in a data warehouse.

True	False	Cannot Say

QUESTION 12 – Corporate memory is an alternative name given to historical data.

True	False	Cannot Say

PASSAGE 5 – WHAT IS A CUSTOMER CHARTER

A Customer Charter is a statement as to how a company will deliver a quality customer service. The main purpose of a Customer Charter is to inform customers of the standards of service to expect, what to do if something goes wrong and how to make a complaint. In addition to this a Customer Charter also helps employees by setting out clearly defined standards of how they should perform within the organisation in relation to customer service delivery.

IS IT NECESSARY FOR AN ORGANISATION TO HAVE ONE?

Whilst not a legal requirement, a Customer Charter is an ideal way of helping organisations define what that service should be and the standard that should be expected. The charter will also help customers get the most from an organisation's services, including how to make a complaint if they are dissatisfied with any aspect of service or if they have ideas for improvement.

OTHER POINTS TO CONSIDER

A Customer Charter should be written in a clear and user-friendly manner. In addition to this, a Crystal Mark endorsement by the Plain English Campaign would enhance its status. If appropriate, it should be displayed in a prominent place, so all customers can see it. The Customer Charter must be available in different formats, such as large print and audio, so that customers with particular needs can access it. If an organisation is part of an industry where a regulator has been appointed, details of how to contact the regulator should be included.

QUESTION 13 - A Customer Charter is a legal requirement within an organisation.

True	False	Cannot Say

QUESTION 14 – A Customer Charter must be written using a Crystal Mark endorsement by the Plain English Campaign.

True	False	Cannot Say

QUESTION 15 – The Customer Charter may be available in different formats, such as large print and audio, so that customers with particular needs can access it.

True	False	Cannot Say

PASSAGE 6 – WHAT IS A BALANCE SHEET

A balance sheet is a snapshot of a company's financial position at a particular point in time. In contrast, an income statement measures income over a period of time.

A balance sheet is usually calculated for March 31, last day of the financial year. A financial year starts on April 1 and ends on March 31. For example, the period between April 1, 2011 and March 31, 2012 will complete a financial year. A balance sheet measures three kinds of variables: assets, liabilities and shareholder's equity.

Assets are things like factories and machinery that the company uses to create value for its customers. Liabilities are what the company owes to third parties (eg outstanding payments to suppliers). Equity is the money initially invested by shareholders plus the retained earnings over the years. These three variables are linked by the relationship: Assets = Liabilities + Shareholder's equity. Both assets and liabilities are further classified based on their liquidity, that is, how easily they can be converted into cash.

Current liabilities are liabilities that are due within a year and include interest payments, dividend payments and accounts payable. Long-term assets include fixed assets like land and factories as well as intangible assets like goodwill and brands. Finally, long-term liabilities are basically debt with maturity of more than a year.

QUESTION 16 - A financial year starts on March 31, the last day of the financial year, and ends on April 1.

True	False	Cannot Say

QUESTION 17 – It can be said that the liquidity of both assets and liabilities is how easily they can be converted into cash.

True	False	Cannot Say

QUESTION 18 – A balance sheet is a legal requirement and every company must have one.

True	False	Cannot Say

PASSAGE 7 – SENDING FRANKED MAIL

You have the option of a one-off collection or a regular daily collection at a pre-arranged time. You can print and complete the form for a regular collection, or if you require a one-off collection or wish to discuss your collection requirements in more detail you can call the Business Relations Manager.

If you need to carry out an urgent same day mailing and would like your mail collected, you'll need to let us know before 12.00pm the same day by calling the Business Support telephone number. We will then arrange a single collection from your premises.

WEEKEND COLLECTIONS: We cannot collect on Saturdays or Sundays without prior arrangement. If you are interested in arranging a weekend collection for your business then please contact your allocated business support manager. A turnover in excess of £2500 per annum is required for this service. Any franked mail inaccuracies will be rejected.

PREPARING FRANKED MAIL FOR COLLECTION

1. Be sure to address your mail correctly, using the correct postcode and postage.
2. Bundle all franked mail together, with the addresses facing the same direction.

3. Bundle different types of mail separately.

4. Put stamped mail in separate bags.

5. Weigh each pouch, bag or tray, checking that they're less than 11kg (to comply with the health and safety limit).

6. Check that all your mail is ready for collection on time and at your collection point.

QUESTION 19 - Saturday collections can be arranged with prior arrangement.

True	False	Cannot Say

QUESTION 20 – The health and safety limit for a bag of mail is less than 11kg.

True	False	Cannot Say

QUESTION 21– Bundled franked mail with the addresses that are not facing the same direction will be rejected.

True	False	Cannot Say

SUGGESTED ANSWERS AND EXPLANATIONS

PASSAGE 1 - WINTER FUEL PAYMENTS

1. You can qualify for a Winter Fuel Payment if you move to France.

Answer - B (FALSE)

Explanation: The passage states "you cannot qualify for a Winter Fuel Payment if you move to another European Economic Area country". The statement is, therefore, false.

2. Winter Fuel Payment can only be paid directly in your bank account.

Answer - B (FALSE)

Explanation: The statement is false because the passage states "Winter Fuel Payment is paid for the household and will be paid directly into your bank account or by cheque depending on which format you requested".

3. Members of the public will not qualify for a winter Fuel Payment if, throughout the week of 19–25 September 2011, they were in a care home.

Answer - A (TRUE)

Explanation: The passage confirms the statement to be true.

PASSAGE 2 – WHITEHAM SUPERMARKET

4. Brownhaven is seven miles from Whiteham.

Answer - C (CANNOT SAY)

Explanation: Based on the information provided in the passage we cannot say whether this statement is true or false.

5. Barry works at the local supermarket on Sundays.

Answer - A (TRUE)

Explanation: The passage confirms that "Barry works every day except Wednesday." The statement is, therefore, true.

6. The town of Redford is four miles from the town of Tenford.

Answer - B (FALSE)

Explanation: The passage states that "The town of Redford is four miles from Whiteham and six miles from the seaside town of Tenford." The statement is, therefore, false based on the information provided.

PASSAGE 3 – FAMILY HOLIDAY

7. Jessica's first choice would be a walking holiday in the hills of their home country.

Answer - B (FALSE)

Explanation: The passage states that Jessica's first choice would be a skiing holiday; therefore, the sentence is false.

8. Janet and Jessica have been married for twenty-seven years.

Answer - B (FALSE)

Explanation: The sentence states that Janet and Jessica have been married, whereas the passage states Janet and Steve. Therefore, the sentence is false.

9. Jessica would rather go skiing than go on a sunny holiday abroad.

Answer - A (TRUE)

Explanation: We can tell from the sentence that Jessica would rather go skiing than go on a sunny holiday abroad as skiing is her first choice. The correct answer is true.

Following the five sample questions you should have a better understanding of how the questions are formatted and also how to approach them. You will have gathered that the most important factor when answering the questions is to totally base your answer on the facts that are provided within the passage.

PASSAGE 4 – DATA WAREHOUSES

10. Integrated and non-volatile data form some of the characteristics of a data warehouse.

Answer - A (TRUE)

Explanation: It is true, according to the passage, that some of the characteristics of a data warehouse include integrated and non-volatile data.

11. It is not possible to identify which employees were on sick leave from the information stored in a data warehouse.

Answer - B (FALSE)

Explanation: It is possible to ascertain which employees were off sick from the information stored in a data warehouse; therefore, the statement is false.

12. Corporate memory is an alternative name given to historical data. Answer - A (TRUE)

Explanation: It is true that corporate memory is an alternative name given to historical data.

PASSAGE 5 – CUSTOMER CHARTER

13. A Customer Charter is a legal requirement within an organisation.

Answer - B (FALSE)

Explanation: The passage clearly states that a Customer Charter is not a legal requirement. The correct answer is false.

14. A Customer Charter must be written using a Crystal Mark endorsement by the Plain English Campaign.

Answer - B (FALSE)

Explanation: The passage states that a Customer Charter should be written in a clear and user-friendly manner and that a Crystal Mark endorsement by the Plain English Campaign would enhance its status. However the use of a Crystal Mark is not compulsory. Therefore, the statement is false.

15. The Customer Charter may be available in different formats, such as large print and audio, so that customers with particular needs can access it.

Answer - B (FALSE)

Explanation: The passage states that "The Customer Charter must be available..." The statement above states that it 'may' be available. Therefore, it is false.

PASSAGE 6 – WHAT IS A BALANCE SHEET

16. A financial year starts on March 31 and ends on April 1.

Answer - B (FALSE)

Explanation: The statement is false because the passage states that a financial year starts on April 1 and ends on March 31. The statement is therefore false.

17. It can be said that the liquidity of both assets and liabilities is how easily they can be converted into cash.

Answer - A (TRUE)

Explanation: The passage clearly states that both assets and liabilities are further classified based on their liquidity, that is, how easily they can be converted into cash. The correct answer is true.

18. A balance sheet is a legal requirement and every company must have one.

Answer - C (CANNOT SAY)

Explanation: The passage makes no reference to this statement; therefore, cannot say is the correct answer.

PASSAGE 7 – SENDING FRANKED MAIL

19. Saturday collections can be arranged with prior arrangement.

Answer - A (TRUE)

Explanation: The passage states that they cannot

collect on Saturdays or Sundays without prior arrangement. Therefore, the statement is true.

20. The health and safety limit for a bag of mail is less than 11kg.

Answer - A (TRUE)

Explanation: The passage indicates that less than 11kg is the health and safety limit; therefore, the correct answer is true.

21. Bundled franked mail with the addresses that are not facing the same direction will be rejected.

Answer - A (TRUE)

Explanation: In paragraph 3 of the passage it states that any franked mail inaccuracies will be rejected. The statement is true.

Civil Service
Verbal Reasoning
Test 3

The following 21 questions are split evenly between 7 sample passages in banks of 3 questions per passage. Your task is to answer each question either true, false or cannot say.

Here's a quick reminder of what is meant by TRUE, FALSE or CANNOT SAY, in the context of a verbal reasoning test.

TRUE - If a statement is 'true', then it can be verified by the text. This means that the text must explicitly or implicitly mention something which proves the statement to be correct. In other words, you cannot make any assumptions about the text. There must either be direct evidence for the statement, or a strong inference to support the statement.

FALSE - If a statement is 'false', there must be evidence in the text which contradicts the statement. For example, if the question statement says 'all swans are white', but the text says 'there is such a thing as a black swan', then the statement is false because it is directly contradicted by the text.

CANNOT SAY - If there is not enough evidence to verify that the statement is true or false, then the correct answer is 'cannot say' Simply put, this means that you cannot say the statement is true or false based on the information provided in the passage.

Civil Service Verbal Test. Practice Test 2

Read the following passages and answer the questions either as **TRUE**, **FALSE** or **CANNOT SAY**

You have 25 minutes to complete the 21 questions.

PASSAGE 1 – ANALYSTS PROVING FORECASTERS WRONG

The Office for National Statistics (ONS) said internet shopping and sales of household goods had been better in October compared with previous months. However, sales of clothing and footwear, where many retailers cut prices before Christmas, were particularly weak.

The increase came as a surprise to many analysts who were predicting a 0.4% fall in internet shopping and sales of household goods. The rise meant that retail sale volumes in the three months leading up to January were up by 2.6% on the previous quarter. The final quarter of the year is a better guide to the underlying trend than one month's figures.

Some analysts cautioned that the heavy seasonal adjustment of the raw spending figures at the turn of the year made interpreting the data difficult. Even so, the government will be relieved that spending appears to be holding up despite the squeeze on incomes caused by high inflation, rising unemployment, a weak housing market and the crisis in the eurozone.

Retail sales account for less than half of total consumer spending and do not include the purchase of cars or eating out. The ONS said that its measure of inflation in the high street – the annual retail sales deflator – fell to 2.2% last month, its lowest level

> since November 2009. Ministers are hoping that lower inflation will boost real income growth during the course of 2012.

QUESTION 1 – Ministers hope that higher inflation will boost real income growth during 2012.

True	False	Cannot Say

QUESTION 2 – Analysts predicted a 0.4% rise in the sales of household goods.

True	False	Cannot Say

QUESTION 3 – The crisis in the eurozone is contributing to the squeeze on incomes.

True	False	Cannot Say

PASSAGE 2 – THE IMPORTANCE OF HEALTH AND SAFETY IN THE WORKPLACE

Employers must protect the health and safety of everyone in your workplace, including people with disabilities, and provide welfare facilities for your employees.

Basic things you need to consider are outlined below.

WELFARE FACILITIES

For your employees' well-being you need to provide:

- Toilets and hand basins, with soap and towels or a hand-dryer, drinking water.
- A place to store clothing (and somewhere to change if special clothing is worn for work).
- Somewhere to rest and eat meals.

HEALTH ISSUES

To have a healthy working environment, make sure there is:

- Good ventilation – a supply of fresh, clean air drawn from outside or a ventilation system.
- A reasonable working temperature (usually at least 16°C, or 13°C for strenuous work, unless other laws require lower temperatures).
- Lighting suitable for the work being carried out.

> - Enough room space and suitable workstations and seating.
> - A clean workplace with appropriate waste containers.

QUESTION 4 – It is the responsibility of the employee for keeping a workplace safe.

True	False	Cannot Say

QUESTION 5 – Providing the employee with a suitable workstation is a consideration for the employer when making the workplace safe.

True	False	Cannot Say

QUESTION 6 – An employer must ensure that all floor surfaces are non-slip in order to prevent slips, trips and falls.

True	False	Cannot Say

PASSAGE 3 – HOW TO ENROL IN OUR ONLINE SELLERS' PROGRAMME

To enrol in our online sellers' programme, you must have an email account, access to the Internet, have a UK distribution facility and also hold the full UK distribution rights to the item(s) you want to sell.

You must have a UK bank account capable of receiving payments via electronic bank transfer (BACS), as this is the only method of payment we offer. Each product you wish to sell in our programme must meet our minimum eligibility standards. These standards relate to quality, value, subject matter, production standards and compliance with intellectual property laws. We reserve the right to remove any products if they do not meet our standards. You are not permitted to sell any products that are deemed to be pornographic or racist.

Any books that you wish to sell via our sellers' programme must have a 10 or 13-digit ISBN number and applicable barcode printed on the back of the book in the bottom right-hand corner.

The barcode must scan to match the ISBN of the book. If the item you want to sell is a music CD then the CD must be in a protective case which meets the relevant British Standard.

The title and artist name must be printed on and readable from the spine (the thin side of the CD). Once again, the CD must contain a barcode which must scan to match the EAN or UPC.

If your item is a DVD or VHS video. Rules that apply to music CDs are also applicable to DVD products.

QUESTION 7 – The barcode on a CD must be printed on the back in the bottom right-hand corner.

True	False	Cannot Say

QUESTION 8 – Pornographic products are permitted in the online sellers' programme.

True	False	Cannot Say

QUESTION 9 – ISBN is short for International Standard Book Number.

True	False	Cannot Say

PASSAGE 4 – WHAT CRITERIA DO WE USE TO DECIDE IF TRADE DISTRIBUTION IS APPROPRIATE?

Firstly, we will only consider a distribution relationship with publishers who have a UK-based storage and representation arrangement. Generally, we will hold a larger stock than would normally be required of a wholesaler, but we do need to have easy access to top-up facilities within the UK.

In addition, it is imperative that the titles are represented to the trade in order to generate UK sales. Whether this is via a UK-based sales/marketing presence, or one based overseas, is not important, as long as it is effective in selling the titles to the target audience. Although we offer some promotional assistance through our weekly/monthly publications we do not offer sales and marketing as a service per se.

MINIMUM TURNOVER/LINES

The publisher should normally be able to demonstrate a realistic expectation of turnover in excess of £50k per annum at RRP and have a minimum of 5 lines. However, these targets are both negotiable where appropriate.

WHAT TERMS WILL BE REQUIRED?

Final discount and credit terms will be agreed on a case-by-case basis. Stock will be held on a consignment basis and we will provide monthly statements of sales and other management information. Invoicing will be against sales achieved each month and within the credit terms agreed.

QUESTION 10 – All invoices are paid 30 days in arrears.

True	False	Cannot Say

QUESTION 11 – An application from a publisher with a turnover of £49k will be accepted.

True	False	Cannot Say

QUESTION 12 – Applicants who reside in southern Ireland will not be considered for a trade account.

True	False	Cannot Say

PASSAGE 5 – LEARNING THE TRAIN DRIVER'S ROUTE KNOWLEDGE

Competence in the train driver's route knowledge is extremely important, simply because trains have such a long stopping distance. As an example, a train travelling at a speed of 200 km/h can take three miles to stop. If the driver lacks route knowledge, then stopping distances can be compromised. Stopping distances can be greatly affected by the weight of a train. Trains cannot be driven on line-of-sight like road vehicles because the driver has to know what is up-ahead in order to operate the train safely. This is why route knowledge is so important to the role of a train driver.

During initial training a trainee driver will be given a Route Learning Ticket. This gives the driver authority to travel in the cab whilst they learn the routes under supervision of a qualified instructor or qualified train driver. However, visual aids such as videos and visual learning platforms are being introduced so that drivers can learn the routes in a more controlled environment.

In order to successfully pass the route knowledge assessment a driver must learn all of the stations, speed restrictions, signals, signal boxes, level crossings, gradients and other features that are applicable to the role.

> The assessment is either with a question and answer session in front of the manager or with a multiple choice route assessment package on a computer.

QUESTION 13 – A train's stopping distance is increased by the weight of the train.

True	False	Cannot Say

QUESTION 14 – A train travelling at a speed of 400 km/h will take six miles to stop.

True	False	Cannot Say

QUESTION 15 – Learning speed restrictions and stations will help towards passing the route knowledge assessment.

True	False	Cannot Say

PASSAGE 6 – THE HISTORY OF FOOTBALL

The earliest records of a game similar to football as we know it today are from China in 206 BC. By AD 500, round footballs stuffed with hair were in use. It is suggested that Roman legions may have introduced the game to Europe and England in particular during the Roman occupation from AD 40 to AD 400.

The game increased in popularity, developing into 'mob games' called mêlées, or mellays, in which a ball, usually an inflated animal bladder, was advanced by kicking, punching and carrying. As many as 100 players from two towns or parishes started at a mid-point and used their localities' limits as goals. King Richard II of England banned the game in 1389 because it interfered with archery practice, and later monarchs issued similar proscriptions into the 15th century, to little effect.

By the middle of the 19th century it was decided that uniformity of the rules was necessary so that every team could play the same game. Therefore the Football Association (FA) was formed in England and during the latter part of 1863, following a series of meetings, the first rules of the game of football were laid down. The first rules were based on those that had been in use at Cambridge University at the time. Some of the first rules also known as the Laws of the Game (there were 14 in total) included:

> Rule 1. The maximum length of the ground shall be 200 yards; the maximum breadth shall be 100 yards; the length and breadth shall be marked off with flags; and the goals shall be defined by two upright posts, 8 yards apart, without any tape or bar across them.
>
> Rule 10. Neither tripping nor hacking shall be allowed, and no player shall use his hands to hold or push an adversary.

QUESTION 16 – By the middle of the 19th century it was decided that uniforms would be worn by referees.

True	False	Cannot Say

QUESTION 17 – King Richard II of England practised archery.

True	False	Cannot Say

QUESTION 18 – According to the passage there were four Laws of the Game.

True	False	Cannot Say

PASSAGE 7 – THE HISTORY OF THE SAS

The Special Air Service was originally founded by Lieutenant David Stirling during World War II. The initial purpose of the regiment was to be a long-range desert patrol group required to conduct raids and sabotage operations far behind enemy lines.

Lieutenant Stirling was a member of Number 8 Commando Regiment and he specifically looked for recruits who were both talented and individual specialists in their field, and who also had initiative.

The first mission of the SAS turned out to be a disaster. They were operating in support of Field Marshal Claude Auchinleck's attack in November 1941, but only 22 out of 62 SAS troopers deployed reached the rendezvous point. However, Stirling still managed to organise another attack against the German airfields at Aqedabia, Site and Agheila, which successfully destroyed 61 enemy aircraft without a single casualty. After that, the 1st SAS earned regimental status and Stirling's brother Bill began to arrange a second regiment called Number 2 SAS.

It was during the desert war that they performed a number of successful insertion missions and destroyed many aircraft and fuel depots in the process. Their success contributed towards Hitler issuing his Kommandobefehl order to execute all captured Commandos. The Germans then stepped up security and as a result the SAS changed their tactics. They used jeeps armed with Vickers K machine guns and used tracer ammunition to ignite fuel and aircraft. When the Italians captured David Stirling, he ended up in Colditz Castle as a prisoner of war for the remainder of the war. His brother, Bill Stirling, and 'Paddy' Blair Mayne, then took command of the regiment.

QUESTION 19 – During the SAS's first mission only 42 of the total troopers deployed reached the rendezvous point.

True	False	Cannot Say

QUESTION 20 – When the Germans captured David Stirling, he ended up in Colditz Castle as a prisoner of war for the remainder of the conflict.

True	False	Cannot Say

QUESTION 21 – Lieutenant Stirling was a member of Number 8 SAS Regiment.

True	False	Cannot Say

SUGGESTED ANSWERS AND EXPLANATIONS

PASSAGE 1 - ANALYSTS PROVING FORECASTERS WRONG

1. Ministers hope that higher inflation will boost real income growth during 2012.

Answer - B (FALSE)

Explanation: The passage states that ministers hope that 'lower' inflation will boost real income growth, not higher. Therefore, the statement is false.

2. Analysts predicted a 0.4% rise in the sales of household goods.

Answer - B (FALSE)

Explanation: The passage states that analysts were predicting a 0.4% fall in sales of household goods, not rise. Therefore, the statement is false.

3. The crisis in the eurozone is contributing to the squeeze on incomes.

Answer - A (TRUE)

Explanation: This statement is true based on the information provided in the passage.

PASSAGE 2 – THE IMPORTANCE OF HEALTH AND SAFETY IN THE WORKPLACE

4. It is the responsibility of the employee for keeping a workplace safe.

Answer - C (CANNOT SAY)

Explanation: The passage makes no reference to this statement. Therefore, we cannot say whether the statement is true or false from the information provided. Cannot say is the correct answer.

5. Providing the employee with a suitable workstation is a consideration for the employer when making the workplace safe.

Answer - A (TRUE)

Explanation: We can deduce from the passage that this statement is true.

6. An employer must ensure that all floor surfaces are non-slip in order to prevent slips, trips and falls.

Answer - C (CANNOT SAY)

Explanation: In health and safety law this statement is true. However, the passage makes no reference it. Cannot say is the correct answer.

PASSAGE 3 – HOW TO ENROL IN OUR ONLINE SELLERS' PROGRAMME

7. The barcode on a CD must be printed on the back in the bottom right-hand corner.

Answer - C (CANNOT SAY)

Explanation: The passage states that CDs require a barcode. However, no reference is made to the barcode location for CDs. Therefore the answer is cannot say.

8. Pornographic products are permitted in the online sellers' programme.

Answer - B (FALSE)

Explanation: The passage clearly states that pornographic products are not permitted. Therefore, the correct answer is false.

9. ISBN is short for International Standard Book Number.

Answer - C (CANNOT SAY)

Explanation: The passage makes no reference to this.

PASSAGE 4 – WHAT CRITERIA DO WE USE TO DECIDE IF TRADE DISTRIBUTION IS APPROPRIATE?

10. All invoices are paid 30 days in arrears.

Answer - C (CANNOT SAY)

Explanation: The passage makes no reference to this statement. The answer is cannot say from the information provided.

11. An application from a publisher with a turnover of £49k will be accepted.

Answer - C (CANNOT SAY)

Explanation: Although the passage makes reference to an expected turnover of £50k per annum, it also states that the targets are negotiable. Because the targets are negotiable, we cannot confirm whether the statement is true or false. As such, we must select 'cannot say' as the correct answer.

12. Applicants who reside in southern Ireland will not be considered for a trade account.

Answer - C (CANNOT SAY)

Explanation: The passage states that they will only consider a distribution relationship with publishers who have a UK-based storage and representation arrangement. Southern Ireland does not form part of the UK. However, the statement doesn't makes reference to applicants who 'reside' in southern Ireland. Because an applicant resides in southern Ireland we cannot say whether or not their application will be considered, simply because there is nothing to prevent a resident of southern Ireland from having a UK-based storage and representation arrangement. Therefore, the correct answer is cannot say from the information provided.

PASSAGE 5 – LEARNING THE TRAIN DRIVER'S ROUTE KNOWLEDGE

13. A train's stopping distance is increased by the weight of the train.

Answer - C (CANNOT SAY)

Explanation: Whilst common sense would dictate that a train's stopping distance will increase by its weight we can only answer the question based on information provided. The passage states that stopping distances can be greatly affected by weight; however, it does not confirm that the stopping distance is increased by the weight. Therefore, we must choose cannot say.

14. A train travelling at a speed of 400 km/h will take six miles to stop.

Answer - C (CANNOT SAY)

Explanation: The passage states that a train travelling at a speed of 200km/h can take three miles to stop. You could be forgiven for assuming that a train travelling at 400 km/h would take six miles to stop. However, the passage does not confirm this and therefore we must select cannot say as the correct answer.

15. Learning speed restrictions and stations will help towards passing the route knowledge assessment.

Answer - A (TRUE)

Explanation: This is made clear by the third paragraph.

PASSAGE 6 – THE HISTORY OF FOOTBALL

16. By the middle of the 19th century it was decided that uniforms would be worn by referees.

Answer - C (CANNOT SAY)

Explanation: Although the passage makes reference to the 19th century and uniformity, it does not make reference to referees wearing uniforms. The correct answer is cannot say from the information provided.

17. King Richard II of England practised archery.

Answer - C (CANNOT SAY)

Explanation: This is a tricky one that may catch some people out! The passage states that King Richard II of England banned the game in 1389 because it interfered with archery practice. However, the passage does not state that it was he who practised archery. Therefore, the correct answer is cannot say.

18. According to the passage there were four Laws of the Game.

Answer - B (FALSE)

Explanation: The sentence is false. The passage states that there were fourteen Laws of the Game.

PASSAGE 7 – THE HISTORY OF THE SAS

19. During the SAS's first mission only 42 of the total troopers deployed reached the rendezvous point.

Answer - B (FALSE)

Explanation: According to the passage only 22 out of 62 troopers deployed reached the rendezvous point. The answer is false.

20. When the Germans captured David Stirling, he ended up in Colditz Castle as a prisoner of war for the remainder of the conflict.

Answer - B (FALSE)

Explanation: The passage states that the Italians captured David Stirling, not the Germans. The correct answer is false.

21. Lieutenant Stirling was a member of Number 8 SAS Regiment.

Answer - B (FALSE)

Explanation: Lieutenant Stirling was a member of Number 8 Commando Regiment, not Number 8 SAS Regiment. The correct answer is false.

Final words

Now you have reached the end of this guide you should now be in a position to sit your Civil Service interview with confidence. A few important things to remember are.

- When applying for any job, you should be planning right from the moment you click the 'Apply' button or register your interest. At How2become we have a simple formula 'Planning' + Practice = 'Prepared'. This should include the following points.
- The job description should provide the basis for your preparation. This will state which of the behaviours you will be assessed against during the selection process. Ensure you understand each of the behaviours fully.
- Study the Civil Service Strengths Dictionary to ensure you have a full understanding of strengths.
- Pay particular attention to the strengths which are related to the behaviours relevant to the role you are applying for.
- Start your interview preparation early, do not wait until you are informed that you have been selected for an interview. This could be at short notice, especially in the current times as many interviews are conducted remotely and can be

scheduled at short notice, so be prepared!
- To have any chance of success you must be prepared, the job market is incredibly competitive with large numbers applying for single vacancies.
- Research the organisation you are joining.

We wish you all the best for your interview.

The how2become team

The How2Become Team

Printed in Dunstable, United Kingdom